OVERPOPULATION

EARTH • AT • RISK

EARTH • AT • RISK

OVERPOPULATION

by Rebecca Stefoff

Introduction by
Russell E. Train

Chairman of
the Board of Directors,
World Wildlife Fund and
The Conservation Foundation

CHELSEA HOUSE PUBLISHERS

new york   philadelphia

CHELSEA HOUSE PUBLISHERS
EDITOR-IN-CHIEF: Richard S. Papale
EXECUTIVE MANAGING EDITOR: Karyn Gullen Browne
COPY CHIEF: Philip Koslow
PICTURE EDITOR: Adrian G. Allen
ART DIRECTOR: Nora Wertz
MANUFACTURING DIRECTOR: Gerald Levine
SYSTEMS MANAGER: Lindsey Ottman
PRODUCTION COORDINATOR: Marie Claire Cebrián-Ume

EARTH AT RISK
SENIOR EDITOR: Jake Goldberg

Staff for *Overpopulation*
COPY EDITOR: Danielle Janusz
EDITORIAL ASSISTANT: Robert Kimball Green
PICTURE RESEARCHER: Villette Harris
SENIOR DESIGNER: Marjorie Zaum

First printing

1 3 5 7 9 8 6 4 2

Library of Congress Cataloging-in-Publication Data
Stefoff, Rebecca.
  Overpopulation/Rebecca Stefoff; introductory essay by Russell
E. Train.
    p. cm.—(Earth at risk)
  Includes bibliographical references and index.
  Summary: Examines the results of demographic changes and
illustrates the threat of overpopulation to man and his
environment.   93 - 18721
  ISBN 0-7910-1581-5
      0-7910-1606-4 (pbk.)
  1. Population—Juvenile literature. 2. Population—Economic
aspects—Juvenile literature. [1. Population.]
I. Title. II. Series.   92-15869
HB883.S74 1993   52441   CIP
363.9′1—dc20   AC

C O N T E N T S

INTRODUCTION

Russell E. Train

Administrator, Environmental Protection Agency, 1973 to
1977; Chairman of the Board of Directors, World Wildlife
Fund and the Conservation Foundation

There is a growing realization that human activities increasingly
are threatening the health of the natural systems that make life possible
on this planet. Humankind has the power to alter nature fundamentally,
perhaps irreversibly.

This stark reality was dramatized in January 1989 when *Time*
magazine named Earth the "Planet of the Year." In the same year, the
Exxon *Valdez* disaster sparked public concern over the effects of human
activity on vulnerable ecosystems when a thick blanket of crude oil
coated the shores and wildlife of Prince William Sound in Alaska. And,
no doubt, the 20th anniversary celebration of Earth Day in April 1990
renewed broad public interest in environmental issues still further. It is
no accident then that many people are calling the years between 1990
and 2000 the "Decade of the Environment."

And this is not merely a case of media hype, for the 1990s will
truly be a time when the people of the planet Earth learn the meaning of
the phrase "everything is connected to everything else" in the natural
and man-made systems that sustain our lives. This will be a period when
more people will understand that burning a tree in Amazonia adversely
affects the global atmosphere just as much as the exhaust from the cars
that fill our streets and expressways.

Central to our understanding of environmental issues is the
need to recognize the complexity of the problems we face and the

relationships between environmental and other needs in our society. Global warming provides an instructive example. Controlling emissions of carbon dioxide, the principal greenhouse gas, will involve efforts to reduce the use of fossil fuels to generate electricity. Such a reduction will include energy conservation and the promotion of alternative energy sources, such as nuclear and solar power.

The automobile contributes significantly to the problem. We have the choice of switching to more energy-efficient autos and, in the longer run, of choosing alternative automotive power systems and relying more on mass transit. This will require different patterns of land use and development, patterns that are less transportation and energy intensive.

In agriculture, rice paddies and cattle are major sources of greenhouse gases. Recent experiments suggest that universally used nitrogen fertilizers may inhibit the ability of natural soil organisms to take up methane, thus contributing tremendously to the atmospheric loading of that gas—one of the major culprits in the global warming scenario.

As one explores the various parameters of today's pressing environmental challenges, it is possible to identify some areas where we have made some progress. We have taken important steps to control gross pollution over the past two decades. What I find particularly encouraging is the growing environmental consciousness and activism by today's youth. In many communities across the country, young people are working together to take their environmental awareness out of the classroom and apply it to everyday problems. Successful recycling and tree-planting projects have been launched as a result of these budding environmentalists who have committed themselves to a cleaner environment. Citizen action, activated by youthful enthusiasm, was largely responsible for the fast-food industry's switch from rainforest to domestic beef, for pledges from important companies in the tuna industry to use fishing techniques that would not harm dolphins, and for the recent announcement by the McDonald's Corporation to phase out polystyrene "clam shell" hamburger containers.

Despite these successes, much remains to be done if we are to make ours a truly healthy environment. Even a short list of persistent issues includes problems such as acid rain, ground-level ozone and smog, and airborne toxins; groundwater protection and nonpoint sources of pollution, such as runoff from farms and city streets; wetlands protection; hazardous waste dumps; and solid waste disposal, waste minimization, and recycling.

Similarly, there is an unfinished agenda in the natural resources area: effective implementation of newly adopted management plans for national forests; strengthening the wildlife refuge system; national park management, including addressing the growing pressure of development on lands surrounding the parks; implementation of the Endangered Species Act; wildlife trade problems, such as that involving elephant ivory; and ensuring adequate sustained funding for these efforts at all levels of government. All of these issues are before us today; most will continue in one form or another through the year 2000.

Each of these challenges to environmental quality and our health requires a response that recognizes the complex nature of the problem. Narrowly conceived solutions will not achieve lasting results. Often it seems that when we grab hold of one part of the environmental balloon, an unsightly and threatening bulge appears somewhere else.

The higher environmental issues arise on the national agenda, the more important it is that we are armed with the best possible knowledge of the economic costs of undertaking particular environmental programs and the costs associated with not undertaking them. Our society is not blessed with unlimited resources, and tough choices are going to have to be made. These should be informed choices.

All too often, environmental objectives are seen as at cross-purposes with other considerations vital to our society. Thus, environmental protection is often viewed as being in conflict with economic growth, with energy needs, with agricultural productions, and so on. The time has come when environmental considerations must be fully integrated into every nation's priorities.

One area that merits full legislative attention is energy efficiency. The United States is one of the least energy efficient of all the industrialized nations. Japan, for example, uses far less energy per unit of gross national product than the United States does. Of course, a country as large as the United States requires large amounts of energy for transportation. However, there is still a substantial amount of excess energy used, and this excess constitutes waste. More fuel-efficient autos and home heating systems would save millions of barrels of oil, or their equivalent, each year. And air pollutants, including greenhouse gases, could be significantly reduced by increased efficiency in industry.

I suspect that the environmental problem that comes closest to home for most of us is the problem of what to do with trash. All over the world, communities are wrestling with the problem of waste disposal. Landfill sites are rapidly filling to capacity. No one wants a trash and garbage dump near home. As William Ruckelshaus, former EPA administrator and now in the waste management business, puts it, "Everyone wants you to pick up the garbage and no one wants you to put it down!"

At the present time, solid waste programs emphasize the regulation of disposal, setting standards for landfills, and so forth. In the decade ahead, we must shift our emphasis from regulating waste disposal to an overall reduction in its volume. We must look at the entire waste stream, including product design and packaging. We must avoid creating waste in the first place. To the greatest extent possible, we should then recycle any waste that is produced. I believe that, while most of us enjoy our comfortable way of life and have no desire to change things, we also know in our hearts that our "disposable society" has allowed us to become pretty soft.

Land use is another domestic issue that might well attract legislative attention by the year 2000. All across the United States, communities are grappling with the problem of growth. All too often, growth imposes high costs on the environment—the pollution of aquifers; the destruction of wetlands; the crowding of shorelines; the loss of wildlife habitat; and the loss of those special places, such as a historic structure or area, that give a community a sense of identity. It is worth noting that growth is not only the product of economic development but of population movement. By the year 2010, for example, experts predict that 75% of all Americans will live within 50 miles of a coast.

It is important to keep in mind that we are all made vulnerable by environmental problems that cross international borders. Of course, the most critical global conservation problems are the destruction of tropical forests and the consequent loss of their biological capital. Some scientists have calculated extinction rates as high as 11 species per hour. All agree that the loss of species has never been greater than at the present time; not even the disappearance of the dinosaurs can compare to today's rate of extinction.

In addition to species extinctions, the loss of tropical forests may represent as much as 20% of the total carbon dioxide loadings to the atmosphere. Clearly, any international approach to the problem of global warming must include major efforts to stop the destruction of forests and to manage those that remain on a renewable basis. Debt for nature swaps, which the World Wildlife Fund has pioneered in Costa Rica, Ecuador, Madagascar, and the Philippines, provide a useful mechanism for promoting such conservation objectives.

Global environmental issues inevitably will become the principal focus in international relations. But the single overriding issue facing the world community today is how to achieve a sustainable balance between growing human populations and the earth's natural systems. If you travel as frequently as I do in the developing countries of Latin America, Africa, and Asia, it is hard to escape the reality that expanding human populations are seriously weakening the earth's resource base. Rampant deforestation, eroding soils, spreading deserts, loss of biological diversity, the destruction of fisheries, and polluted and degraded urban environments threaten to spread environmental impoverishment, particularly in the tropics, where human population growth is greatest.

It is important to recognize that environmental degradation and human poverty are closely linked. Impoverished people desperate for land on which to grow crops or graze cattle are destroying forests and overgrazing even more marginal land. These people become trapped in a vicious downward spiral. They have little choice but to continue to overexploit the weakened resources available to them. Continued abuse of these lands only diminishes their productivity. Throughout the developing world, alarming amounts of land rendered useless by overgrazing and poor agricultural practices have become virtual wastelands, yet human numbers continue to multiply in these areas.

From Bangladesh to Haiti, we are confronted with an increasing number of ecological basket cases. In the Philippines, a traditional focus of U.S. interest, environmental devastation is widespread as deforestation, soil erosion, and the destruction of coral reefs and fisheries combine with the highest population growth rate in Southeast Asia.

Controlling human population growth is the key factor in the environmental equation. World population is expected to at least double to about 11 billion before leveling off. Most of this growth will occur in the poorest nations of the developing world. I would hope that the United States will once again become a strong advocate of international efforts to promote family planning. Bringing human populations into a sustainable balance with their natural resource base must be a vital objective of U.S. foreign policy.

Foreign economic assistance, the program of the Agency for International Development (AID), can become a potentially powerful tool for arresting environmental deterioration in developing countries. People who profess to care about global environmental problems— the loss of biological diversity, the destruction of tropical forests, the greenhouse effect, the impoverishment of the marine environment, and so on—should be strong supporters of foreign aid planning and the principles of sustainable development urged by the World Commission on Environment and Development, the "Brundtland Commission."

If sustainability is to be the underlying element of overseas assistance programs, so too must it be a guiding principle in people's practices at home. Too often we think of sustainable development only in terms of the resources of other countries. We have much that we can and should be doing to promote long-term sustainability in our own resource management. The conflict over our own rainforests, the old growth forests of the Pacific Northwest, illustrates this point.

The decade ahead will be a time of great activity on the environmental front, both globally and domestically. I sincerely believe we will be tested as we have been only in times of war and during the Great Depression. We must set goals for the year 2000 that will challenge both the American people and the world community.

Despite the complexities ahead, I remain an optimist. I am confident that if we collectively commit ourselves to a clean, healthy environment we can surpass the achievements of the 1980s and meet the serious challenges that face us in the coming decades. I hope that today's students will recognize their significant role in and responsibility for bringing about change and will rise to the occasion to improve the quality of our global environment.

A view of the earth from space is a dramatic reminder that the human environment is finite and limited. The planet cannot continue to provide adequate resources for an ever-growing number of people.

chapter 1

IS THIS THE WAY
THE WORLD ENDS?

Suppose that somehow your radio could pick up transmissions from the future—a news broadcast from the year 2025. What would the leading news stories be? Some of them might sound like this:

- At latest count, 60 nations are experiencing critical food shortages. Millions of men, women, and children—most of them in Africa, Latin America, and South Asia—are starving. Experts say that benefit concerts by all the rock bands in the world would not even begin to make a dent in the appalling famines that have become a way of life in these tortured countries.

- India and Pakistan have gone to war over the precious trickle of water that still flows down the cracked, sun-baked bed of the Indus River. Most of Pakistan is desert. Every drop of water is urgently needed to slake the thirst of its rapidly growing population and to irrigate its fields, although each year's harvest is smaller than that of the year before. India's rivers and wells used to be replenished each year by the torrential monsoon rains, but weather patterns have changed because of tropical deforestation and global warming, climatologists say. As a result, India's monsoon rains are lighter than they used to be, and sometimes they do not come at all. If the monsoons ever fail two years in a row, say Indian leaders and economists, half a billion people will face starvation. Both India and Pakistan are wracked by suffering, torn by internal strife, and increasingly desperate to control the Indus River. Both possess nuclear weapons. Observers fear a repetition of the water wars that broke out during the past decade between Egypt and Ethiopia over the Nile River, and between Mexico and the United States over the Rio Grande.

- In the United States, a guerrilla group from the Pacific Northwest has claimed responsibility for dynamiting the pipeline that was recently built to drain water from the Northwest to the parched fields and orchards of California, where watering lawns and washing cars have just been made criminal offenses. In the American Southwest, the Colorado River, which has been steadily shrinking, appears to have dried up completely this week. Environmentalists blame its disappearance on the scores of irrigation and water diversion projects that have been built along the river's course, including the new $4.2 billion Grand Canyon Dam and Power Plant. The state of Arizona has just passed a tax increase to help pay for the water that it must import from Canada. Meanwhile, Canada has announced that its supply of exportable water, in the form of pieces of ice cut from its glaciers, is good for only another 18 years. The Canadian government is expected to announce an increase in the price of water shortly.

◦ The U.S. government, which established nationwide water rationing last year, is now considering proposals to take control of all food stocks and begin food rationing as well. In a related story, the nations of Europe and the Russian Commonwealth have once again called for international action to force the United States to resume grain exports, which were suspended three years ago during the last major worldwide drought.

◦ The federal government has authorized the use of U.S. Army helicopter units to patrol the highways that lead into the centers of 16 major cities. These cities are surrounded by America's worst shantytowns—huge slums with no electricity or paved roads, densely packed with dwellings made out of trash and old cars. Some cities in Europe are also planning to introduce military protection for their major highways, which are now guarded only by electrified fences. Both American and European shanty dwellers have become increasingly unmanageable, and highway piracy is now common on the outskirts of most cities.

◦ This bulletin just in from Central Africa: a 6-month, 10-nation research project has failed to find any wild animals in this part of the continent. Similar searches are planned for Southeast Asia and South America, if funds for them can be found, but it is now thought that all wildlife in these regions is extinct. A few wild animals are known to survive, however, in the two national parks that have been preserved in the United States.

None of these news stories is true—yet. Perhaps none of them will ever be true. Together they paint a nightmarish picture of the future, a portrait of a world that no one would want to inhabit. Yet each of these stories is a possibility; each *could* happen. And each of them is related to another item that probably *will* be a news story in 2025. That story concerns overpopulation. In mid-1991, there were about 5.4 billion people on earth. That year the world's population increased by more than 95 million. The global *birth rate* was 27 and the *death rate* was 9, according to the Population Reference Bureau (PRB) in Washington, D.C. This means that for every 1,000 of the earth's inhabitants, 27 people were born and 9 people died. Another way to put it: for every person who died, three were born. The total population was growing fast enough to double its size in 40 years. Experts in population studies at the PRB and elsewhere say that if present trends in growth continue, by 2025 the world will be home to 8.6 billion people.

The world is already feeling the pressure of human population growth, which has placed an enormous strain on the environment and also on the ability of nations to feed and house their citizens. Many people feel that the earth is now overpopulated, that it already has too many human inhabitants. According to this view, the earth's resources are stretched to the limit just to support the current population of 5.4 billion people. If the global population does reach 8.6 billion by the year 2025, it is almost certain that the resources available for those people—food, jobs, places to live, and medical care—will not increase sufficiently to provide decent lives for all of them. Even in 1991, 34% of the world's population lived in extreme poverty, defined by the United Nations as being too poor to buy enough food to stay healthy or work productively. Another 50% of the world's people got by on less food than the average American ate. Many people in this group also lacked things that most Americans and other Westerners routinely enjoy: things such as an adequate supply of clean water for drinking and washing, regular medical care, and electrical appliances and the energy that powers them.

Human population growth will do more than add to the problem of meeting people's basic needs. It will affect the whole

World population in the 20th century has been growing geometrically, that is, at an ever increasing rate.

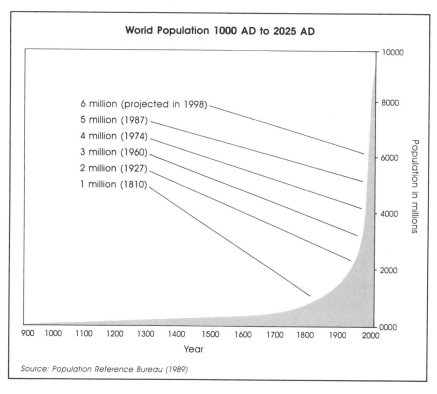

World Population 1000 AD to 2025 AD

6 million (projected in 1998)
5 million (1987)
4 million (1974)
3 million (1960)
2 million (1927)
1 million (1810)

Population in millions

900 1000 1100 1200 1300 1400 1500 1600 1700 1800 1900 2000

Year

Source: Population Reference Bureau (1989)

planet. Many of today's most serious environmental problems—including global warming, the destruction of tropical rainforests, and air and water pollution—are directly related to the number of people on the planet. As that number increases, these and other environmental problems are bound to get worse.

THE THIRD ROAD

The 20th-century British poet T. S. Eliot wrote these lines in his poem "The Hollow Men":

This is the way the world ends
Not with a bang but a whimper.

In their 1990 book *The Population Explosion*, biologists Paul Ehrlich and Anne Ehrlich used these lines to describe two dire fates that could overtake civilization. The "bang" is global nuclear warfare. For much of the 20th century it seemed as though the world might indeed end in just such a horrific bang. Global nuclear conflict, it was predicted, would destroy civillization as it is now known. The death tolls would be enormous: Millions would die in the initial direct hits and the firestorms that would follow. Millions more would die in the following months and years, some from radiation sickness and others from starvation brought about by worldwide climate disruption—the so-called nuclear winter. Some studies of the possible outcomes of nuclear war suggested that humanity might be utterly wiped out.

At the beginning of the 1990s, the threat of nuclear war appeared to be growing more distant. Communism collapsed in

Eastern Europe and the Soviet Union, and the Soviet superpower was replaced by a Commonwealth of Independent States. The long-standing enmity between the United States and the old Soviet Union was evolving into a new, less hostile relationship, and the world's superpowers began cautiously reducing their stockpiles of nuclear weapons. These were hopeful signs, although the nuclear threat was by no means ended. But while there may now be less reason to fear immediate nuclear destruction, the world appears to have moved closer to Eliot's other fate, the "whimper."

If the bang is a sudden, fiery cataclysm, the whimper is a slow, lingering sickness. Its symptoms are the growing degradation of the earth's natural environment, the rising rate of forest destruction and wildlife extinction around the planet, and the increasingly frequent outbreaks of famine and disease among the populations of the world's poorest and most crowded countries.

In the whimper view of the end of the world, these conditions will continue to worsen steadily while the human population climbs at an accelerating rate. Soon the developing countries will be haunted by mass starvation, plague, and the breakdown of all order. Civil wars and international wars over resources will break out in all parts of the world. Even in developed nations such as the United States, the quality of life will deteriorate dramatically because of smog, chronic water shortages, skyrocketing food prices, perpetual traffic gridlock, widespread unemployment, bankrupt educational and health-care systems, crowding, urban crime, and the high incidence of "environmental" illnesses such as skin cancer from sun exposure. Eventually, order will break down in the United States, Japan, and

A rapidly growing population pressing on limited resources will affect society in many ways. Traffic congestion and the breakdown of transportation systems are among the results of unplanned growth.

other prosperous, industrialized nations, and civilization will deteriorate into packs of scavengers scrabbling to survive in a ruined world.

The bang packs an unthinkable amount of suffering and death into a few short days or months. The whimper draws it out over many years, perhaps a century or more. But the long-term prospects for humanity are bleak in both versions. Either way, the world of human life and experience that T. S. Eliot knew—and that most people today know—will end.

But the bang and the whimper are certainly not human-ity's only choices. There are other possible futures as well, prospects that offer the hope not just of survival but of improving the health of the environment and the lives of people around the world. The bang and the whimper are two roads that humanity might follow, but there is a third road. That road is change—change in the way humans view the world and each other. Preservation and protection, rather than consumption and de-struction, could become the driving motives not just of scattered individuals but of corporations, governments, and all of society.

Is such change possible? Neurobiologist Robert Ornstein and population biologist Paul Ehrlich think that it is. Their 1989 book *New World, New Mind* claims that humanity is now at "its most important turning point." Say Ornstein and Ehrlich, "For the first time humanity has the knowledge to destroy itself quickly, and for the first time humanity also has the knowledge to take its own evolution into its hands and change now, change the way people comprehend and think." One of the most crucial changes that people can make is to begin thinking about population and how it relates to the health of humanity and the world, now and in the future.

In Bangladesh, people left homeless by a devastating cyclone surround relief workers as they await emergency food aid. Rapid population growth in Third World countries puts an enormous burden on available resources and thwarts plans for economic development.

chapter 2

THE POPULATION
EXPLOSION

Human beings, or their direct ancestors, have lived on this planet for several million years. If people have been around for such a long time, how does it happen that their population is growing so rapidly today? Why was the earth not overpopulated long ago? The answer lies in the kind of life that humans lived for many thousands of years before recorded history began.

Anthropologists—scientists who study people and their cultures—have pieced together a picture of prehistoric human life from several sources. One source is the traces left by the people of the distant past—traces such as bones, tools, and cave paintings. But a great deal has also been learned by studying the few small groups of people who even today live in much the same way that early human cultures lived.

The Khoisan people of Africa's Kalahari Desert (formerly called the Bushmen), as well as certain isolated rainforest tribes in Borneo and the Amazon Basin, are what anthropologists call hunter-gatherers. That is, they obtain their food and the other necessities of life by hunting wild animals and gathering wild grains, fruits, nuts, eggs, edible plants and insects, and honey.

They do not farm, and they do not keep domestic animals. They are nomads; instead of living in one place they move from place to place, although their wanderings are generally not aimless but follow a pattern shaped by the seasons, by tribal tradition, or by agreements with other groups.

The needs of hunter-gatherer communities are simple: food, water, shelter, clothing or ornaments, tools, and medicine. Hunter-gatherers get everything they need from nature: animals, edible plants, herbs, leaves, vines, trees, bones, skins, ashes, and stones. These materials are the resource base of the community.

The population of a hunter-gatherer community does not grow rapidly. Rather, it stays much the same over long periods of time. This is because, when the group starts to become too large for its resource base to support it properly, people begin to die—generally the youngest children and the old people, who are most vulnerable to disease and hunger. Some primitive societies have been known to kill infants and old people, or to allow them to die of exposure, in times of famine or drought. To the modern mind such practices seem cruel, but to hunter-gatherer societies they are survival strategies for emergency situations, designed to keep alive the strongest, most productive members of the tribe.

For the most part, however, hunter-gatherer communities keep their populations small by regulating fertility, or the number of children that women have. One way they do this is by spacing births widely. Having no access to dairy milk or to processed baby formula or food, women generally nurse their children for two or three years or even longer; during this time they usually do not become pregnant. The result is that a woman will not begin devoting her resources of food and energy to a new baby until her older child has survived the perils of early childhood. In some hunter-gatherer cultures, custom and tradition limit family size. Other customs may confine people's sexual activity to certain seasons or conditions.

For countless generations, the ancestors of modern humans were hunter-gatherers. They lived in many of the habitable parts of Africa and Asia, but the population of each nomadic group remained stable and fairly small. Death from food shortages, predatory animals, exposure, or illness was common.

Population is determined by the interplay of two factors. One is the birth rate, or the number of people being born, and the other is the death rate, or the number who die. The difference between the two is called the rate of *natural increase*. If the birth rate is greater than the death rate, the rate of natural increase is a positive number—that is, the population is growing larger. But if the death rate is greater than the birth rate, the rate of natural increase is a negative number, and the population is shrinking. Over several million years of early human history, birth and death rates were about the same. The population remained stable, or grew extremely slowly. Then came three revolutionary changes in the way human beings lived and multiplied.

THREE REVOLUTIONS

The first of these great changes can be called the Evolutionary Revolution. It occurred during the most recent of the world's major ice ages, 100,000 years ago or even earlier, when *Homo sapiens*, the modern human species, appeared. The other early human forms soon disappeared, leaving the earth to *Homo sapiens*, who spread out to fill it.

With the arrival of the modern species, the population of humans began to grow. The new people made stone and bone tools that were more effective than those of the earlier humans. They formed larger, more culturally elaborate communities, and they also began trading tools, artworks, and other goods between groups. Hunting took on a larger place in their lives, as men used improved weapons and team tactics to bring down big game such as bison and woolly mammoths. People were still hunter-gatherers, but because they were hunting on a much larger scale their overall food supply increased, and so did their population.

By about 10,000 years ago, the last Ice Age was drawing to an end. The huge ice sheets that had covered much of Europe, North America, and northern Asia began to shrink. Water from the melting glaciers raised the level of the oceans. Plants and animals that were adapted to life along the cold fringes of the glaciers withdrew, like the glaciers themselves, to chilly mountain peaks high above sea level or to the north. At the same time, plants and animals that favored warmer, milder weather were able to expand into plains and valleys that had formerly been covered with ice and snow. Based on the distribution of skeletons and other traces left by communities, scientists believe that the human population totaled about 5 million.

It was at this time, roughly 8000 B.C., that humanity underwent its second great change, the Agricultural Revolution. Farming was developed in the Middle East, where the earliest farmers grew wheat, barley, beans, and fruit, and in Southeast Asia, where agriculture was based on rice. A few thousand years later, several Native American peoples independently developed agricultures based on corn, beans, squash. People also began to domesticate grazing animals such as cattle, sheep, and goats.

For the first time, humankind was able to cultivate a dependable food supply in a settled location of its own choosing. The first villages and towns were born, and endless wandering was no longer the way of life for everyone. Also for the first time, communities were able to harvest and store more food than they needed for immediate consumption. This meant that communities could feed more people than ever. Birth rates went up and families got larger.

The Agricultural Revolution sped up the rate at which humans were increasing their numbers all over the world. By 2,000 years ago, some 6,000 years after the Agricultural Revolution began, the world population probably totaled 200 to 300 million. It had taken all the millennia from the origin of humankind until 8000 B.C. for the population to reach 5 million. But in just 6,000 years after the discovery of farming, the 5 million had multiplied by at least 4,000%.

The human population continued to grow a little faster each century. Population growth was not perfectly steady; there were setbacks, such as the outbreaks of bubonic plague—called the Black Death—that killed a quarter to a third of the people of Europe during the 14th century. But by 1650 the world population had reached 500 million, or half a billion. And a century after that came the Industrial Revolution, which transformed human life for the third time.

The Industrial Revolution began when people began digging peat and coal for use as fuel. Later, petroleum and natural gas were harnessed. New energy sources led to new uses for energy, such as factories and railroads, and eventually automobiles, the chemical and plastics industries, and automated industry. The Industrial Revolution also dramatically sped up the rate of natural increase by lowering the death rate—in other words, by allowing people to live longer.

In 1750, at the dawn of the Industrial Revolution, *life expectancy* at birth was 25 years. This meant that the average baby born in 1750 could expect to live for about that long. The *infant mortality rate* was 400, which meant that 400 out of every 1,000 babies died before their first birthday. But among the technological advances spawned by the Industrial Revolution were modern sanitation, pest-control chemicals, and medicine. Death rates dropped in countries where people had access to these benefits, first in Europe and North America, later in parts of Asia, Latin America, and Africa. Many infectious diseases were brought under control, and medical treatment began to lengthen the lives of people with chronic diseases such as cancer. Life expectancy increased; infant mortality decreased. By 1991 the average life expectancy was 65 years, and the infant mortality rate was 68 per thousand births.

Lower death rates—fewer people dying each year in relation to the number being born—meant a huge jump in total population. The population of Europe and North America grew rapidly in the 19th century as death rates dropped. In the 20th century, these continents' population growth dropped when *fertility rates* decreased—people were having smaller families. The total number of people in Europe and North America continued to increase, but it increased more slowly. By this time death rates in the less industrialized world had also decreased dramatically. As a result population growth skyrocketed in Asia and Latin America, reaching a peak in the 1960s. The rate of growth later slowed a little in Asia and Latin America; since the 1970s Africa has had the fastest-growing population.

The Industrial Revolution did more than usher in a period of rapid population growth. It also changed the geographical *distribution* of the population—that is, how people were concentrated or spread out across the land. The world's cities had long been the seat of government, trade, and the arts. During the Industrial Revolution they also became hubs of mass transportation and centers of industry. In the 19th century, cities such as London and New York and Tokyo mushroomed when people moved to the city from the countryside in search of jobs in the new factories. Before long the population of the cities was

A newspaper engraving of a factory district in Germany in the mid-19th century. The technological advances of the Industrial Revolution reduced both the rate of infant mortality and the death rate of older persons, enabling more people to live longer.

growing much faster than that of the rural districts; some rural areas even shrank in population for a while because of migration to the cities.

The change from a mostly rural population to a predominantly city-dwelling population, with the accompanying rapid growth of the cities, is called urbanization. It began with the Industrial Revolution and continues today. Urbanization is one of the most important characteristics of population growth in the late 20th century. Cities around the world are growing fast, and urban population is increasing faster than rural population in almost every country.

In 1950, about 29% of all people lived in cities, and seven cities had populations of 5 million or more. In 1991, 43% of the world's people lived in cities, and the number of cities with populations greater then 5 million had jumped to 35. Experts at the United Nations and the Population Reference Bureau predict that by the year 2000, 17 cities will have more than 10 million people. Many of these cities will be in the developing nations of the Third World, where some of today's fastest-growing cities are located. Mexico City, with a population of 22 million, is expected to have 26 million inhabitants by the end of the 20th century; São Paulo, Brazil, will have 24 million; and Bombay, India, will have 16 million. Throughout the Third World, the population growth rate of cities is twice the overall population growth rate. In terms of worldwide population distribution, half of the world's inhabitants—some 3 billion individuals—will be city dwellers in the year 2010.

Environmental damage is another trend that accelerated during the Industrial Revolution. People today often think that the degradation of the earth's natural environment by human activity is strictly a modern problem, but it is not. Past generations have also mismanaged and damaged their environments. Philosophers in ancient Greece worried about people causing soil erosion by cutting down too many of the trees in that mountainous country. The ancient Chinese also suffered from deforestation, which contributed to water runoff, floods, and droughts. The air and water of early Rome were dangerously polluted.

But environmental destruction has proceeded on an even larger scale and at a faster rate ever since people started burning fossil fuels during the Industrial Revolution. Oil spills in pristine seas, automobile exhaust forming smog umbrellas over cities, chlorofluorocarbon gases (CFCs) that destroy ozone in the atmosphere, toxic waste from the manufacture of plastics and chemicals, landfills clogged and water sources polluted by those same plastic and chemical products—these are some results of the Industrial Revolution that humankind has not yet learned to control. These problems and a host of others are closely related to population growth, which keeps making every problem larger and harder to solve.

THE SNOWBALL EFFECT

A pattern is clearly visible in the growth of the earth's population over time. According to researchers at the Population Reference Bureau, the earth's population reached 1 billion in the year 1800, 2 billion in 1930, 3 billion in 1960, 4 billion in 1975, and 5 billion in 1987. This means that although it took hundreds of thousands of years for global population to reach its first billion, it took only 130 years to add the second billion, 30 years to add the third billion, 15 years to add the fourth billion, and 12 years to add the fifth billion.

This rapid growth shows no sign of stopping soon. Using information about current rates of population growth gathered by the United Nations and the World Bank, in 1991 the Population Reference Bureau projected that world population would reach 6 billion in 1998, 7 billion in 2009, 8 billion in 2020, 9 billion in 2033, and 10 billion in 2046.

If human population growth had increased at a steady rate—adding, for example, 1 billion people every 200,000 years—the graph representing growth would be a straight line slanted upward. Instead the graph is a sharply rising curve. This pattern is called exponential growth. Exponential growth starts slowly, but after a time it suddenly picks up speed. Enormous jumps in growth can occur quite rapidly. Population experts often illustrate exponential growth with a "twenty-ninth day" example. Suppose a weed starts growing on the surface of a pond. The weed doubles its size every day. After 29 days, the weed covers half the pond. But just one day later the pond is completely covered—and the fish die.

Human population growth has also been described in terms of the "snowball effect." If a small snowball starts rolling down a hill, it gathers up more snow as it goes. The more snow it picks up, the faster it rolls, and the faster it rolls, the more snow it gathers. Both its size and its speed can increase quite quickly. Human population growth has snowballed. As the human population grew larger, its rate of growth picked up speed, and it kept growing faster and faster, until by 1991 it was growing so fast that it was as though another New York City were being added to the world's population every month.

No snowball can keep rolling and growing forever. It will probably be blocked by a snowdrift or roll to a halt on a stretch of level ground. But sometimes, if a snowball gets big enough and fast enough, it turns into an avalanche—an enormous, swiftly moving wall of snow that can engulf and destroy whole towns.

POPULATION SCIENCE

Over the centuries, people have held a variety of views about population size. Many ancient societies, including the Roman Empire, were *natalist*—that is, they encouraged marriage and high fertility. They believed that large populations equaled power and success.

This early pronatalism was echoed in a school of thought called mercantilism, which arose after Europe was ravaged by bubonic plague in the Middle Ages. According to mercantilism, a nation's population was a resource. The larger the population, the richer the nation. Frederick II, who was king of Prussia (now Germany) from 1740 to 1786, expressed this view when he said, "The number of the people makes the wealth of states." The mercantilists did not worry about overpopulation; they believed that any population, whatever its size, could produce enough food and other necessities to sustain itself.

In the 18th century, the mercantilists came under attack from the physiocrats, a group of thinkers who claimed that land, not people, was the basis of economic production. Unlike the mercantilists, the physiocrats did not believe that unlimited

The English economist Thomas R. Malthus (1766–1834), who argued that populations will tend to outgrow their food supply and then suffer catastrophic reductions as a result of famine and disease. Some of Malthus's followers became early advocates of birth control.

population growth would increase wealth. They thought, instead, that it would lead to widespread poverty and suffering. From the tradition of the physiocrats came the work of Thomas Malthus, who produced one of the first systematic studies of population. Malthus published his *Essay on the Principle of Population* in 1798 and continued to refine and revise it until his death in 1834. In it he argued that populations have a natural tendency to outgrow their food supplies. A population eventually becomes too big for its resource base, and then famine, war, and disease will impose population limits. To avoid such disasters, Malthus felt that society's laws and customs should encourage limits on reproduction and population size. Some of Malthus's followers in later generations led movements to make information about birth control available to the public.

Since the 19th century, the study of population has developed into a scientific discipline called *demography.* Its experts are demographers; they gather and study statistics about the size and distribution of populations, and about how the sexes and age groups are represented within each population. These statistics are called *demographics.*

Demographics reveal the *fertility rate,* birth rate, death rate, natural increase, average life expectancy, and infant mortality rate of populations. Two other important demographic factors that are often used in discussions of population growth are *doubling time,* which is the time it would take a given population to double its size if its current rate of growth continued unchanged, and *replacement reproduction rate,* which is the fertility rate at which each couple in a given population is replaced by two descendants, so that the total number of people stays the same over the long term.

But demographers are increasingly aware that the study of population is not simply an abstract collection of numbers. Vital political and economic issues are closely tied to the size and distribution of the population. Demographers now draw upon a variety of disciplines, such as history, biology, economics, and sociology; they also in turn contribute demographic insights to these disciplines. One of the closest links is between demography and ecology, the study of the relationships between creatures and their environments. Demographers and ecologists alike are warning that the explosive growth of the human race is threatening the health of planet Earth itself.

Schoolchildren in a Czechoslovakian village wear respirators to protect themselves from industrial air pollutants.

chapter 3

GLOBAL ECOSYSTEM BREAKDOWN

Ecologists use the term *carrying capacity* to refer to an environment's long-term ability to support its inhabitants. An aquarium for guppies, a prairie with herds of grazing cattle, a planet occupied by people—every environment has a carrying capacity, or limit. A population that exists within the limit of its environment's carrying capacity is called sustainable. Sustainable populations do not require more resources than their environments can provide, and they do not damage the long-term health or productivity of their environments.

But if a population exceeds the environment's carrying capacity, either by increasing its numbers or by increasing its use of resources (or both), the environment begins to suffer. Resources are degraded to the point where they are no longer useful or used up faster than they can be replaced. If there are too many guppies in an aquarium, their waste fouls the water. The aquarium's delicately balanced environment becomes disordered. The guppies must compete for food, oxygen, and living space. Eventually they kill each other, or they begin to sicken and die. If there are too many cattle grazing on a prairie, they eat up the grass cover faster than it can regrow. Without grass to hold it in place, the topsoil blows away, reducing the prairie's fertility. Less grass grows each year, and the prairie slowly turns into a desert. Its carrying capacity declines. The cattle grow gaunt, vulnerable to disease and starvation, and each year the prairie can support fewer of them.

Like the aquarium and the prairie, the earth itself is an environment with a carrying capacity. In recent years it has become all too clear that the global environment is suffering a number of serious disorders. Many scientists believe these disorders are a signal that humanity has reached its carrying capacity—or has already gone beyond it.

The earth is a complex network of physical systems. Photosynthesis turns sunlight and nutrients into energy in green plants. The hydrological cycle moves water from cloud to rainfall to evaporation and back to cloud. Wind and water currents, climate and weather, the proportions of different gases in the atmosphere, the manufacture of soil by bacteria and earthworms—all of these are interconnected to form a single global ecosystem. That ecosystem provides people with certain essential services: food, water, breathable air, and temperatures suitable for life. But there are ominous signs that the ecosystem is undergoing severe strain and may be on the verge of a breakdown. The symptoms of that strain are a host of environmental problems, all connected in some way to population size.

GLOBAL WARMING

Global warming is a rise in the earth's overall temperature because of an increase in certain greenhouse gases in the atmosphere. These gases—notably carbon dioxide and methane—trap the sun's heat as it radiates off the earth's surface. Without the greenhouse gases, all the sun's heat would escape into space, and the earth would be frozen and lifeless. But if there is too much greenhouse gas in the atmosphere, the amount of heat that it traps will accumulate, turning up the temperature all over the world about 10 times faster than the warming that occurred at the end of the last ice age.

Certain human activities have released greenhouse gases into the atmosphere, especially since the Industrial Revolution. Wood, coal, petroleum, and natural gas contain carbon. When they are burned, carbon dioxide enters the atmosphere. Automobile exhausts, forests burned to clear ranch land, and the smokestacks of factories and utility plants all produce large quantities of carbon dioxide. The burning of forests is particularly critical, because living trees absorb carbon dioxide from the air and release oxygen, which animals breathe. When forests are burned, not only does the burning add carbon dioxide, but fewer trees are available to exchange carbon dioxide for oxygen.

Scientists are not yet in full agreement about the rate of global warming, or even about whether it has yet begun. Variations in climate occur naturally, and the earth has experienced many periods of colder and then warmer weather. The warming trend that has been recorded in the 20th century could be part of such a natural cycle. But scientists do agree that if the amount of greenhouse gases in the atmosphere continues to increase, unnatural global warming is unavoidable.

How hot will it get? No one knows. But even minor increases in the earth's average temperature could have widespread effects. People will need more air-conditioning, which will use more energy, which will accelerate the warming. Polar ice will start to melt, and ocean levels will rise. Low-lying coastal lands—such highly populated areas of the world as Florida, the Nile River delta, and the nation of Bangladesh—will be flooded. Coastal wetlands will also be flooded, which could destroy populations of birds and fish. Worldwide weather patterns will change. More rain will probably fall at the poles and the equator; less rain will fall in the world's temperate zones, where most food crops are grown. Food production will become uncertain. Drought, poor harvests, and famine are likely to occur on a devastating scale.

Energy use around the world is growing even faster than population size. Rich nations such as the United States lead the way, using carbon-based energy on a grand scale both in industry and in personal consumption. The people in poorer nations, yearning to copy the energy-rich American way of life, scramble to catch up. All of this energy use is responsible for more than half of all the greenhouse gases added to the atmosphere each year. Most of the rest comes from the burning of forests. A smaller population would use less energy and put less pressure on forests. A larger population would make global warming even harder to prevent.

ACID RAIN

Acid rain is caused by certain types of air pollution—specifically sulfur and nitrogen oxides from automobile exhausts and industrial smokestacks. These pollutants can be carried from their sources along the jet streams of the upper atmosphere for great distances. Eventually, however, the particles fall back to earth with rain (or snow, hail, or dust). Rain that contains these pollutants is more acidic than uncontaminated rain—sometimes so acidic as to sting the skin or eyes of people who get wet. Rainfall with an acidity equal to that of lemon juice has been recorded in the mountains of West Virginia.

Acid rain upsets the balance of both water and woodlands. Thousands of lakes and vast stretches of forestland in industrialized nations such as Sweden, Germany, Canada, and the United States have been damaged by acid rain. Scandinavian lakes that were once full of fish are now completely lifeless. Germany's Black Forest, located in one of the world's most heavily industrialized countries, has lost more than a third of its trees to acid rain. The Germans have coined the word *Waldsterben* (forest death) to describe the ravages of acid rain, but Waldsterben is taking place in many other countries as well.

As with global warming, acid rain is clearly linked both to population size and to Western-style industrialization. But it is not limited to the industrialized nations of the developed world. In remote regions of China acid rain has been caused by the burning of coal for heating and cooking, and in tropical Africa by the burning of forests to clear land for farming. The effects of acid rain in the developing nations can only become more severe as urbanization and industrialization increase in these areas.

DESERTIFICATION

Desertification occurs when fertile land is turned into infertile desert. It is a clear sign that the population of a region has exceeded that region's carrying capacity.

When vegetation is destroyed by too much livestock grazing on it, or by people cutting it down faster than it can regrow, desertification occurs. Much of the southwestern United States, an area of sparsely vegetated semidesert, was lush grassland not long ago, but it has been badly overgrazed by cattle. Erosion is another cause of desertification; it occurs when topsoil is carried away by wind or water because the natural plant cover has been destroyed, or because farmers have used techniques not suited to the local environment. Farmland is sometimes desertified as a result of the very irrigation that made the soil productive in the first place. Irrigation can also waterlog the soil, flooding it with so much water that crops cannot grow. Or irrigation may cause salinization, in which mineral salts from the water build up in the soil. Both waterlogging and salinization can make soil infertile, and desertification results.

Some desertification occurs naturally, but most of it is the result of human activities—and population size plays a major role in this process. More people need more land, more firewood, and more food, putting more and more pressure on ecosystems that may be delicately balanced. The world's most serious desertification problems are found in places with large, fast-growing populations: China, India, and Africa, especially the part of Africa called the Sahel, which lies along the southern edge of the Sahara Desert.

In the mid-1980s the United Nations Environment Program (UNEP) estimated that "moderate" desertification had occurred in about 13 million square miles of the earth's surface; this land—nearly four times the area of the United States—had lost up to 25% of its productivity. Another 6 million square miles of land was "severely" desertified and had lost 50% of its productivity. Satellite photographs reveal that more land has been desertified since then. Each year about 82,000 square miles of the earth's surface—an area equal in size to the state of Kansas—is made useless by desertification. Southern and central Asia, the western United States, southern South America, and parts of Australia appear to be increasingly affected. According to UNEP, as much as one-fifth of the United States (not including

In northern Kenya, too many tribespeople trying to graze too many cattle on too small an area of land have gradually turned the land into desert.

Alaska and Hawaii) has been desertified or is threatened by desertification.

DEFORESTATION

Deforestation, or the permanent loss of forest cover, is a good example of how ecological issues are related to each other and to the size of the human population. A great deal of the earth's original forest cover has already been cut down, and what remains is vanishing fast. The Population Institute and the United Nations estimate that half of all the remaining forests will be destroyed by the year 2000. Forests everywhere are falling to the axe and the torch, but the most serious threat is to the tropical rainforests, especially in Brazil, Indonesia, and Zaire. These rainforests are being destroyed at the rate of 100 acres a minute, or 52.6 million acres a year.

Deforestation is closely connected to several pressing environmental issues. It is related to global warming through forest burning and the loss of carbon-fixing trees. It is a major cause of erosion and desertification; without trees, topsoil readily blows away, or is washed away. Stripping land of trees also changes how water flows over the land. When vegetation covers the land, rainfall is absorbed by a spongy layer of tree roots and the topsoil they hold in place. It then trickles through layers of topsoil and rock into springs, streams, and natural underground reservoirs called *aquifers*. Water sources are thus restored. But when the forest cover is removed, rainfall runs off without being absorbed. This runoff worsens erosion and sometimes causes floods. And when streams and aquifers are not replenished by rainfall, water shortages, droughts, and crop failures may result.

One of the world's worst cases of deforestation has occurred during the past century in the Asian countries of India and Nepal, where most people use firewood for cooking and heating. The expanding population has cut down forests faster than they can renew themselves. The problem is particularly acute in the north, in the foothills of the Himalaya Mountains. The terrain here is steep, and once it has been deforested, its topsoil is quickly washed away. Farming becomes more difficult; floods and landslides become more common. The Himalayas are now so severly deforested that millions of tons of topsoil are washed down their slopes each year.

Deforestation is also related to the extinction of species. According to biologist Edward O. Wilson of Harvard University, each year 10,000 to 17,500 species of plants, birds, insects, reptiles, and mammals vanish forever. Each species is adapted to life in a particular kind of environment, or habitat. When that habitat is tampered with or destroyed, the survival of the species is endangered. All natural habitats are under seige today: deserts, prairies, wetlands, inland waterways, and the seas. But the greatest concentration of species—more than half of all living species—is in the world's tropical rainforests, which are rapidly being destroyed. The crisis of extinction is therefore most desperate in the tropics.

Population size is directly linked to deforestation in a number of ways. As population grows, trees are cut down or burned to make way for new farms, highways, cities, and suburbs. Trees are logged to provide timber for building and pulpwood for newspapers and books. The greater the number of people, the greater the demand for these goods. But the never-ending search for fuelwood in the developing countries of the Third World is,

The more people there are, the greater the demand for wood products for home construction, furniture, fuel, books, newspapers, and packaging materials. All this contributes to extensive deforestation.

according to Werner Fornos, president of the Population Institute, "the single most important cause of deforestation." In 1989 the United Nations Food and Agricultural Organization (FAO) declared that 70% of all families in the developing nations, more than 2 billion people worldwide, rely on firewood as their only fuel. All this wood chopping has tragic consequences. Environmentalist Erik P. Eckhom claims that "the famine in Africa has its origins in erosion and soil degradation resulting from deforestation in the search for firewood."

For thousands of years people have harvested firewood in a sustainable way, leaving enough trees standing to provide a continuing source of wood for the future. But now, in many parts of the world, so many people use firewood every day that trees are being used up faster than they can replace themselves. Entire forests are being leveled. The FAO estimates that by the year 2000 at least half of the developing world will be unable to meet its firewood needs from a sustainable supply. In other words, a huge part of the world's population will have to destroy its resource base in order to obtain fuel, sending the future up in smoke to cook today's meal.

THE POPULATION CONNECTION

There are other signs that the global ecosystem is overloaded and beginning to break down. Both air and water are polluted in many regions—so much so that breathing the air or drinking the water can cause disease. The American Lung Association says that air pollution from automobile exhausts causes 30,000 deaths each year in the United States alone; smog and pollution are even worse in some other nations. And although the U.S. Congress passed a new Clean Air Act in October 1990, the improvements in air quality under the terms of the act will probably be offset by the addition of more cars as the population grows. In 1991 there were 147 million cars in the United States, but the U.S. Environmental Protection Agency estimates that by 2010 that number will have increased by 76%. Each car will contribute less pollution under the new laws, but there will be so many more cars that overall air quality may not improve at all.

Pollution also threatens the oceans. For thousands of years, people thought that the seas were big enough to absorb anything and not be affected. But the discharge of billions of tons of treated and untreated sewage, of toxic industrial waste, and of spilled petroleum is taking its toll. Much of the pollution in the oceans comes from cities and towns that empty waste into the sea and allow construction in the coastal wetlands. This pollution is unlikely to go away; seacoasts are the most densely inhabited parts of the world, and their populations are growing fast. In 1991 more than half of the world's population lived within 60 miles of a seacoast. Demographers expect that as population continues to rise, the percentage of people living near the seacoasts will also rise.

It would be a mistake to think that global warming, deforestation, and other environmental problems are caused *only* by population growth. Most threats to the earth's environment would not disappear entirely even if the total number of people were smaller. There would still be oil spills on the high seas, for example, if the earth had fewer inhabitants but some of them craved an energy-rich life-style based on fossil fuels. And a smaller world population would not guarantee an end to global warming or deforestation. Even if there were fewer people, they might persist in misguided or destructive policies of economic development and environmental mismanagement. But a reduction in population, or even a stabilization and an end to constant growth, would affect the whole range of environmental problems in a positive way. Environmental degradation would almost certainly continue—but it would probably be slower, giving governments and individuals more opportunities to take corrective action.

Population growth has contributed to every threat to the global ecosystem. Continuing population growth will make each problem more severe—and much harder to solve. Biologists who worry about rainforest extinctions, sports fishermen and recreational hikers who want to preserve "the great outdoors," agricultural experts who see fertile topsoil eroding around the world, environmentalists who predict large-scale climate change because of global warming, doctors who fight to save patients with cancers caused by smog or toxic waste—all these and more have begun to see the network of connections that link population to every aspect of the global ecosystem. There is a saying among population scientists that sums up the population connection: "Whatever your cause, it's a lost cause—unless we come to grips with overpopulation."

Years of drought and famine have etched suffering and resignation into the faces of this Ethiopian family.

chapter 4

THE FOOD AND
WATER CRISES

It is possible, although horrible, to imagine people living in a world with no forests, no wildlife, and no rivers or beaches fit for swimming. But it is impossible for people to live without food and water. Yet the world's supply of these necessities is gravely threatened by burgeoning population growth.

In the years after World War II, worldwide grain production almost tripled. Grain—including rice, wheat, corn, oats, barley, and other cereal grasses—is the most commonly used measure of food supply and food production because grains are the basis of everyone's diet, whether they are consumed directly or fed to livestock. Between 1950 and 1984, the total grain production each year exceeded the rate of population growth. The amount of food was growing faster than the number of people.

Several factors caused this boom in food production. For one thing, new land was brought under cultivation. According to Lester Brown of the Worldwatch Institute, the total acreage devoted to raising grain around the world increased by 24%

between 1950 and 1981. Much of this expanded farmland was in China, the former Soviet Union, and the United States.

Another reason for the big increase in food production was a revolution, one that agricultural experts and social planners call the Green Revolution. From 1950 until about 1975, scientists in the United States and other industrialized nations were busy developing new methods of farming to get the highest possible crop yield from every acre. The key to the Green Revolution was the special hybrid varieties of crop plants that were bred to produce high yields. These high-yield plants generally require a lot of fertilizer and chemical pesticides in order to perform at their best. They often need additional irrigation, too.

Through international aid programs, the industrialized nations spread the Green Revolution around the world, with sensational results. Crop yields everywhere increased year after year. There was a mood of hope and optimism as agricultural scientists and government agencies began to believe they could finally feed the world's hungry masses. Technology appeared to be winning the long and bitter battle against starvation. Then the downturn began.

In the mid-1980s grain production leveled off. Then grain output dropped 5% in 1987 and another 5% in 1988, partly because of severe droughts in China, Canada, and the United States. Since then, world grain production has remained stable or has declined slightly; it has not returned to the high levels achieved in the early 1980s. There are several reasons for the slowdown in grain production. The Green Revolution's victories were costly. Many Third World farmers found them-selves unable to afford more and more fertilizers and pesticides. Furthermore, when they *are* used, these chemicals contribute to the degradation of the soil and the entire environment. Excessive irrigation has also caused problems.

The methods of the Green Revolution emphasized high yields in the short term, but they are not well suited to long-term, sustainable agriculture. They have actually damaged cropland in some parts of the world. Desertification, pollution, erosion, and salinization of soil have taken much formerly fertile cropland out of production. Land has also been removed from agricultural use by construction and development. In the United States alone, 3 million acres of cropland are turned into housing estates, shopping malls, and highways each year. China annually loses 4,000 square miles of cropland to con-struction. Many environmentalists and agricultural specialists fear that even worse problems may lie ahead for farmers. Global warming, in particular, could bring sweeping changes in climate and rainfall patterns that might drastically reduce crop yields.

The slowdown in grain output appears even more serious when each year's total grain production is divided by the number of people on the planet. This per-person grain production has fallen each year since 1984 because world population is now increasing much faster than world grain production. Food production in some parts of the world declined even before the global average fell. Per-person grain output has fallen by 10% in Latin America since 1981, by 24% in India since 1983, and by 22% in Africa since 1967.

HUNGER, HEALTH, AND FOOD DISTRIBUTION

All over the world people suffer from lack of food. Every year 40 million to 60 million people in developing countries die of hunger or diseases related to hunger. Malnutrition—which occurs when people do not have enough food, or when their food does not supply them with vital nutrients—causes such diseases as pellagra, anemia, beriberi, rickets, and kwashiorkor. In addition, malnourished people often have faulty immune systems, which makes them ready victims of infectious diseases such as influenza, tetanus, diphtheria, measles, and tuberculosis.

One poignant result of malnutrition and food shortages is that many babies, particularly in developing nations, are victims of low birth weight syndrome. They are born under-weight, which makes them weak and vulnerable to illness. In countries with high infant mortality rates, many of the deaths are due to low birth weight. And even those children who live may suffer from stunted physical or mental growth.

The United Nations estimates that at least 1 billion of the world's inhabitants do not get enough food to allow them to stay healthy and work normally. About 20 million of those underfed people live in the United States; the rest are scattered around the world, with hunger being most concentrated in the Indian Subcontinent—India, Bangladesh, and Pakistan—and in Africa south of the Sahara Desert. Some food-supply experts view Africa's crisis as the most critical. Since 1970 the continent has undergone prolonged, widespread famines. More than 5 million African children died of hunger-related causes each year during the 1980s.

It is sometimes said that people starve because of unequal distribution of food, not because of insufficient production—in other words, the earth produces enough food to feed all of its present inhabitants, if only food were shared equally among all. There are even some who believe that the earth could support a much larger population. In 1988, for example, a group of Roman Catholic bishops declared that the earth could feed 40 billion people. But the bishops' estimate was based on outdated research and information that is now known to be incorrect. The earth could feed 40 billion people *only* if every acre of flat land on its surface were as productive as an acre on a model farm in Iowa— a state of affairs that would be impossible even if environmental degradation did not already threaten much *existing* farmland. The more optimistic estimates of the earth's carrying capacity are based on similarly unrealistic notions or inaccurate data.

Distribution does, however, play a very real part in today's hunger crisis. It is undeniable that most North Americans and Western Europeans are, by the standards of the Third World, overfed. It is also true that people who are now hungry would be able to eat if food were equally available to all rather than being unevenly distributed around the world as a result of agricultural, climatic, political, economic, and social factors. A report issued by Brown University's World Hunger Program states that if all the world's vegetable and grain crops—including the grain that is now fed to livestock—were evenly distributed, there would be enough food to feed 6 billion people a basic vegetarian diet. This would not only support the present global population of 5.4 billion but would allow for a little population growth. But if the diet were improved somewhat, with 15% of total calories coming from animal products such as meat, milk, and eggs, the food supply would sustain only 4 billion people—far fewer than already inhabit the planet. And if the diet were improved even further, with 25% of total calories from animal products, only 3 billion people could be fed—little more than half the present population.

It is clear that the amount of meat people eat has a pronounced effect on the number who can be fed. It takes anywhere from 3 to 16 pounds of grain or legumes (such as soybeans) in the form of livestock feed to produce 1 pound of meat. Grain-fed beef is the most inefficient form of animal protein, requiring 16 pounds of grain for each pound of beef; poultry and eggs require 3 or 4 pounds of feed per pound of animal protein. Because the American diet has traditionally included much more animal protein (and fat) than the world average, the United States is a very inefficient user of grain and legumes. Livestock eat 10 times as much grain as people do in the United States.

On average, the same amount of basic food energy, derived from sunlight through the photosynthesis of plants, can produce a single 2,000-calorie meal of meat or processed foods, or 10 2,000-calorie vegetarian meals. People concerned about world hunger and about the state of the environment often say that Westerners should learn to "eat low on the food chain"—to eat more grains and vegetables and fewer animal products. An extra benefit is that such a diet meets the standards set by the American Heart Association and other medical groups for reducing the risk of such health problems as heart disease, obesity, and colon cancer.

Many aid organizations have made it their goal to eliminate world hunger through more equal distribution of food.

The goal is a noble one. Improved food distribution would undoubtedly end much human suffering. Yet adjustments in food distribution cannot be seen as a long-term solution to the problem of hunger. Population growth would soon intervene. Even if the most efficient farming methods were adopted worldwide, if global warming and the environmental degradation of croplands were halted, if the well-fed nations switched to vegetarian diets, and if all food were shared equally, the demand for food would very soon exceed the supply.

THE WATER OF LIFE

Like food, fresh water is essential to life. And like food, water is unevenly distributed around the world. Some areas are chronically dry and must import water—through pipelines or by channeling it from rivers—to support their populations. But the demands people place upon the world's water supply are increasing rapidly, even faster than the rate of population growth. Between 1950 and 1980, worldwide water use more than tripled; in the United States it increased by 150% during that 30-year period, although the country's population grew by only 50%. In 1990 the United States used about 400 billion gallons of water each day—more than any other industrialized nation. A typical American family of four people used 243 gallons each day; three-quarters of this amount was used in the bathroom.

People use water in three basic ways: domestically, for drinking, cooking, bathing, washing, and sanitation; in industry, mostly for cooling or cleaning processes in factories and power plants; and in agriculture, for irrigation. Of these uses, agriculture is the biggest. Irrigation accounts for 73% of all fresh water use around the world and for more than 80% of water use in the United States. Poorly managed irrigation, however, can cause waterlogging and salinization of the soil, while runoff of chemical fertilizers and pesticides contributes to water pollution.

Furthermore, irrigation is often inefficient. As much as 70% of the water used may not even reach the crops. And a great deal of irrigation is directed at comparatively inefficient activities, such as growing livestock feed (half of all the fresh water used in the United States is consumed for feeding and watering livestock). In California, for example, the livestock industry uses one-seventh

On the Ethiopia-Somalia border, this woman has dug deep into a dried-up river bed to find some brackish water for her family and her goats.

of the state's water but contributes only one five-thousandth of the state's income, according to water analyst Marc Reisner, who has studied water-use policies in the American West. This is possible because the federal government has built dams and other projects that supply water to farmers and ranchers throughout the West at prices well below the water's real cost. For example, in 1981 the U.S. Government Accounting Office reported that farmers who grew cattle feed with water from a $500 million project near Pueblo, Colorado, were paying seven cents for a quantity of water that cost $54 to produce. Another study by the U.S. Bureau of Reclamation—which keeps water prices artificially low—reveals that if water were priced more realistically it would be used more sparingly, and irrigation could become up to 20% more efficient.

Industry uses less water than agriculture—about 21% of the total world water use. But industrial use is responsible for a much higher level of water pollution, especially from dangerous chemicals such as mercury and chlorine. Domestic use accounts for only 6% of all water use, but its impact on the quality of people's lives is great. The Population Institute reported in 1990 that 1.7 billion people, nearly a third of the world's population, did not have an adequate supply of clean drinking water. Three billion people, more than half the total population, lacked adequate sanitation (either flush toilets, sewers, sewage treatment plants, or alternatives such as efficient and safe waste collection). In many places, raw sewage is discharged directly into supplies of drinking or irrigation water.

Health and water are closely related. According to the United Nations World Health Organization (WHO), approximately 80% of all human disease is related to unsafe

continued on page 62

HELL IN THE SAHEL

The Sahel is a wide strip of Africa that runs along the southern fringe of the Sahara Desert. From Mauritania on the west coast of Africa, the Sahel sweeps across the countries of Mali, Burkina Faso, Niger, Chad, Sudan, and parts of Nigeria, Ethiopia, and Somalia. Unlike the Sahara, the Sahel is not a true desert. It is a semidesert region that receives anywhere from 10 to 30 inches of rainfall a year, enough to support hardy seasonal grasses and a few small, tough trees and shrubs.

For centuries the principal economic activity of the Sahel has been livestock herding by nomadic peoples who move with their herds from one feeding ground to another. In the 20th century, however, the number of settled villages and towns has increased, and agricul- ture— culture—especially the growing of peanuts and other cash crops to sell as exports—has become more important, although the Sahelian soil and climate are not well suited to farming.

The 1950s and 1960s were a period of unusually high rainfall in the Sahel. During this fortunate time, cash farming expanded, and the populations of the Sahelian countries skyrocketed. In Niger, for example, the population went from 2.5 million to 3.8 million in the 14-year period from 1954 to 1968, and the area devoted to peanut farming more than tripled. Meanwhile, as more of the land was converted to farms, the nomadic herders were pushed north into new areas, where they found enough vegetation to support their cattle. Their herds got larger and larger. It seemed that progress and prosperity were coming to the Sahel.

Unfortunately for the Sahelians, this burst of growth was based on a temporary, unreliable increase in rainfall. Native traditions warned that periods of high rainfall were followed by droughts, and they were right. In 1968, the Sahel entered a 20-year drought. Suddenly, every- thing dried up. The nomadic herdspeople were the hardest hit. The spread of agriculture had pushed them onto lands that were too un- dependable to sustain them during the drought, and the rapid population growth among both people and cattle had greatly exceeded the carrying capacity of the marginal terrain. People burned every bush and tree for fuel. Starving cattle, camels, and goats ate every scrap of vegetation. The wind began carrying the soil away in enormous clouds. Millions of

60

animals and more than 250,000 people died in the famine that followed. It was at this time that people in the Western world were familiarized with television reports and appeals for help showing gaunt, huge-eyed, hungry children gazing bleakly out from a dusty landscape.

Much of the Sahel has been in the grip of famine ever since, dependent upon food imports and donations. Its towns and cities are choked with refugees fleeing from starvation in the countryside. The population of Nouakchott, Mauritania's capital, soared from 20,000 in 1960 to more than 350,000 in 1987. Sahelian cities, however, were not equipped for such influxes. Many of the newcomers live in slums, on the edge of survival.

Even when rainfall increased somewhat in the late 1980s, matters were not greatly improved. The lack of vegetation to capture the rainfall means that much of the water quickly runs off, carrying what remains of the fragile topsoil with it. A region that was once semiarid grassland, able to support a modest population of people and animals, has become sterile desert. Overpopulation—rapid expansion into an ecosystem that simply cannot sustain so much growth—is to blame.

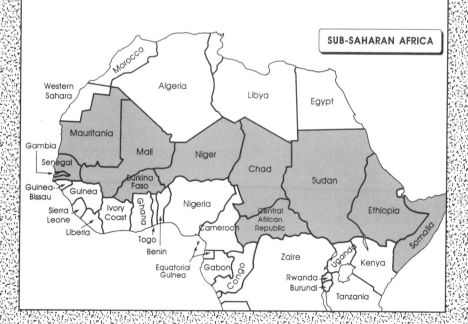

SUB-SAHARAN AFRICA

continued from page 59

drinking water and poor sanitation. In Africa alone, 250 million people, more than a third of the continent's population, will contract water-borne diseases during the 1990s. Contaminated water—with human waste as the major pollutant—carries such viral and bacterial diseases as cholera, typhoid, dysentery and other diarrheal illnesses, polio, elephantiasis, trachoma blindness, and infectious hepatitis. Unsafe water also carries hookworm, tapeworm, and other parasites, including those that cause schistosomiasis, and a variety of crippling diseases. Cancer and neurological diseases have been caused by water polluted with toxic chemicals such as lead, chlorinated solvents, mercury, and polychlorinated biphenyls (PCBs).

Even if all the water now in use were safe, however, that would not guarantee that everyone would have enough water. The supply of fresh water is not endless. There is a limited amount of fresh water in the world, and water that has been contaminated with pollutants is no longer suitable for most uses. Water that drains into the ocean cannot be used for farming or drinking until it has evaporated, condensed into water vapor, and fallen as rainfall; unfortunately, the places that receive the most rainfall are not the places that most urgently need it. Surface water sources, such as rivers and lakes, are replenished fairly steadily if rainfall is regular, but groundwater sources, or aquifers, are replenished so slowly that they must be considered nonrenewable resources, like oil and coal.

There are ominous signs that people are using up their water supply faster than it can be replaced by the rainfall cycle (which may itself be changing because of global warming). One of the most crucial water problems is the draining of aquifers. These vast underground reservoirs were filled by natural processes over many thousands of years. Today they are being emptied at a far faster rate. For example, wells in the Gaza Strip, between Israel and Egypt, draw water from the Gaza Aquifer. Demands on the wells in the crowded Strip have depleted the aquifer by more than 50%. And the water from the wells is getting saltier and saltier because, as the level of fresh water in the Aquifer drops, salt water seeps in from the nearby Mediterranean Sea. The aquifer is now irreversibly contaminated. Such contamination is common when aquifers near bodies of salt water are allowed to become depleted.

Another trouble spot is the Ogallala Aquifer under the American Great Plains. This aquifer supplies groundwater to one-fifth of all the cropland in the United States. Natural replenishment raises the water level in the aquifer by about half an inch every year—but pumping water out for irrigation lowers it four to six feet every year. By the late 1980s the aquifer had been half emptied. No one knows for certain when the aquifer will run dry, but when it does, the effect on American agriculture will be far-reaching and unpleasant. To make matters worse, aquifers sometimes collapse after they are drained. The collapse of the underground chambers not only causes sinkholes and settling in the land above but also means that the aquifer can never be refilled.

During periods of drought, people in California, Nevada, Arizona, New Mexico, Florida, and Texas have experienced water shortages. They have been asked not to fill their swimming pools, water their lawns, or wash their cars. Some cities have introduced water rationing, in which each household is allocated a certain amount of water during the shortage. Many Americans in these drought-prone regions fear that water shortages will become more common, that water rationing will become a way of life. They are almost certainly right. Yet people in other parts of the world experience far greater inconveniences in connection with water.

In many countries people cannot get drinking water in their homes but must line up at public taps. In Madras, India's fourth largest city, the taps flow only between 4:00 A.M. and 6:00 A.M., and people must line up during the night in order to get water. As many as 8,000 rural villages in India have no water supplies at all; each day the village women must walk for miles to the nearest well or stream. Many African women also carry their water jugs across miles of countryside every day to fetch water. In Mexico City, which has 22 million people and very little rainfall, the water level in the city's main aquifer drops by 11 feet each year. The city's vast population of impoverished shanty dwellers must buy what water they can afford from vendors.

In the dry plains of central Asia, farming is possible only with extensive irrigation. Throughout much of the 20th century, irrigation with water drawn from the Caspian Sea and the Aral Sea—both landlocked freshwater lakes rather than true seas—allowed the Soviet Union to increase farm production in its central Asian republics. But the drain for irrigation also caused both lakes to shrink dramatically; the Aral Sea has shrunk by more than 65% since 1960. Now that the Soviet Union has broken up, some economists predict that competition for water from the dwindling lakes could lead to fighting among the newly independent republics.

"Water wars" are a possibility elsewhere as well. Egypt worries that Ethiopia will build dams on the upper reaches of the Nile River. Such dams would mean reservoirs and power plants for the Ethiopians, but they could also mean trouble for the Egyptians downstream, who rely on the Nile for all of their water and also for most of their electric power. The Turkish government is building 21 dams on the upper reaches of the Tigris and Euphrates rivers to bring electricity and irrigation water to parched southeastern Turkey. But the project could cut the amount of Euphrates water that flows into Syria by 40% and the amount that flows into Iraq by 80%. *Al-Ahram*, a Cairo newspaper, called the project "a death sentence over all of Syria and part of Iraq" and "a clear threat to Arab security."

Water is a grave problem—and a source of potential conflict—throughout the Middle East, where water reserves are stretched to their limits to support a regional population of 200 million (expected to increase to 440 million by the year 2020). In 1990 the leaders of 11 Middle Eastern states declared that "water security in the Arab world is as essential as national and military security." Indeed, people in many areas are soon likely to become more desperate for water than for any other resource. The Population Institute's Werner Fornos said in 1991, "The water crises of the 1990s will make the oil crises of the 1970s pale in comparison."

The water crisis is already real in many countries. Part of the problem is unsafe water. There are ways to solve this problem by using existing technology to provide clean drinking water and basic sanitation where they are needed, and by enacting and enforcing strict laws against all forms of water pollution.

The other part of the problem, the shortage of water, is not so easy to solve. On the individual level, people in the United States and other industrialized countries must learn to waste less water. For example, they can install toilets and shower heads

This is not sub-Saharan Africa but the Gibraltar Reservoir near Santa Barbara, California, after four years of drought.

designed to save water, or plant their lawns with vegetation adapted to the local climate so that watering will not be necessary. On the national and international level, governments must develop long-term policies to cut down on water waste, to preserve the groundwater aquifers, and to cooperate in regional water-use projects. But all of these actions, while they are vitally important, cannot add to the earth's finite supply of fresh water. The demand for water will grow as the earth's population grows, and there will be less to go around. Even if everyone on earth starts using water as efficiently as possible, the demand will outgrow the supply—if it has not already done so.

In 1975, 19 countries in the developing world did not have enough renewable water resources for basic domestic uses and irrigation. By 2000 that number is expected to reach 29. By 2025, at least 37 nations will be experiencing severe water stress. Economic development and growth will be impossible in these nations—mere survival will be a challenge. In the late 1980s the World Health Organization claimed that 80 countries, home to 40% of the world's population, were already experiencing some degree of water shortage—perhaps a hint of the great drying that is to come. Says Joyce Starr of the Global Water Summit Initiative, "With global population accelerating toward 12 to 14 billion in the 21st century, maintaining dwindling water supplies and averting contamination must be viewed as strategic priorities."

Pittsburgh, Pennsylvania, in the late 19th century. Rapid industrial growth to fulfill the needs of a growing population has intensified environmental problems such as air pollution, acid rain, and global warming.

chapter 5

S O C I A L   A N D
P O L I T I C A L   P R E S S U R E S

Population size is linked to a host of social, political, and economic factors that shape people's daily lives. As population increases, these factors are likely to exert even more pressure on regions, nations, and individuals.

Public health is closely related to population. Countries with large or rapidly growing populations are crowded, especially in giant cities such as Mexico City and Bombay, and densely crowded areas are breeding grounds for disease. Illnesses caused by lack of sanitation, such as cholera and typhus, often originate in urban slums and spread swiftly through large segments of a population. Epidemiologists (scientists who study the spread of disease) warn that areas of high population increase, particularly where many people are malnourished or lack proper sanitation and health care, are vulnerable to disease epidemics.

It is sometimes said that epidemics, tragic as they are, at least have the effect of reducing the population. This is not the case. The population of Europe fell sharply in the wake of the bubonic plague of the 14th century, but afterward the population grew so swiftly that it soon surpassed its former level. In the

1890s, 6 million people died in India in an outbreak of bubonic plague; a century later, India is one of the world's most populous nations, home to 16% of the world's population. One of the worst epidemics of modern times was the influenza epidemic that swept the world in 1918–19. It killed 20 million people, but nonetheless world population continued to skyrocket during the 20th century. An even greater catastrophe occurred in China between 1958 and 1962, when 30 million people died in a famine. Just 30 years later, China had 1.1 billion people—the largest population of any country—and the government had introduced strict policies to slow the rate of population growth.

Recent years have seen the spread of the deadly disease AIDS (acquired immune deficiency syndrome) around the world. In central Africa, where the disease is most prevalent, it is estimated that 7% to 25% of the population is infected with HIV, the virus that causes AIDS. There is at present no cure for AIDS. If the spread of AIDS is not quickly and effectively controlled through public education and universal adoption of safe sex habits, death

This engraving shows Europeans of the 14th century dancing and praying for divine protection from bubonic plague. Though plagues and epidemics cause much suffering and death, in the long run they are ineffective at controlling population growth.

tolls from the disease are certain to rise for some time. Yet even very high death rates will have little long-term effect on the growth of a global population that is increasing by nearly 100 million every year. As Paul Ehrlich and Anne Ehrlich report in *The Population Explosion*, "While AIDS *could* turn out to be the global epidemic that brutally controls the population explosion by raising death rates, the strains of the virus that have so far been observed seem not to have that capacity." It is more likely that AIDS—like bubonic plague, cholera, typhoid, and influenza—will bring misery and death to millions of men, women, and children, without stopping population growth.

In 1979 the Overseas Development Council measured infant mortality, life expectancy, and literacy around the world for the Physical Quality of Life Index (PQLI). As reported in David Morris's book *Measuring the Condition of the World's Poor*, the PQLI showed that countries with low birth rates had lower rates of infant mortality, longer life expectancies, and greater percentages of people who could read and write. Countries with high birth rates, on the other hand, had high rates of infant mortality, shorter life expectancies, and smaller percentages of literate people. The PQLI suggested that individuals in countries where the population was growing rapidly had less chance of survival than those in countries with slower-growing populations. The 1979 findings still hold true. Two examples: In 1991 Japan's birth rate was 10, the lowest in Asia (the continentwide birth rate was 30). Infant mortality in Japan was 4.5, and life expectancy was 79 years. At the other end of the spectrum, the birth rate in Sierra Leone was 48 (Africa's continentwide rate was 44). Infant mortality in Sierra Leone was 147, and life expectancy was 42 years.

Japan and Sierra Leone differ dramatically in another way as well. According to the Population Reference Bureau's 1991 World Data Sheet, Japan's per capita gross national product (GNP) for 1989—its total economic production divided by its population—was $23,730, the third-highest in the world (only Switzerland's and Luxembourg's were higher). Sierra Leone's per capita GNP for the same year was $200. Japan is one of the richest nations in the world, Sierra Leone one of the poorest. Poverty, *net population growth*, and public health are intertwined. In *The Population Explosion*, Paul Ehrlich and Anne Ehrlich wrote, "Because of the scale of the problem—it involves at least a billion people—it would not be unfair to call poverty the greatest public-health problem today."

In general, birth rates are highest in the poorer Third World countries and lowest in the industrialized nations of Europe. Poverty appears to go hand in hand with high birth rates and rapid population growth. But does rapid population growth cause poverty, or does poverty cause rapid population growth? Some say that population growth causes poverty because, when population growth is rapid, individuals and nations must spend all their resources on the struggle to stay alive. They cannot save money, improve their standard of living, or invest in the future. Others claim that poverty causes overpopulation because poor people, who depend on children to earn money and to care for them in their old age, have large families; in addition, poor people are often uneducated and do not know how to control family size, or they may be unable to afford birth control supplies. But as the Ehrlichs point out, "the 'does population growth cause poverty or vice versa' argument is counterproductive if the goal is to provide everyone with a decent life. If that is the goal, then all of us should be working very hard to end both poverty and population growth, not wasting our efforts trying to determine which causes which."

Not everyone agrees that population, poverty, and health are connected. In his 1981 book *The Ultimate Resource,* economist Julian Simon argues that population growth and crowding have not been proven to have a negative effect on health, life expectancy, or general well-being. (The Netherlands is one of the world's most densely populated countries, for example, and also one of the healthiest.) Simon promotes the theory that economic growth depends upon continued population growth, and that more people will simply mean more minds to develop creative new solutions to the world's problems. But Simon's arguments have not convinced many environmentalists and population scientists that endless population growth is desirable. It is hard to guess how many more creative, innovative minds can flourish in a world short of food, schools, and jobs.

Another way to look at the connection between population and the quality of life is the Index of Human Suffering, developed in 1987 by the Population Crisis Committee (PCC) of Washington, D.C. It measures 10 factors of human welfare in the areas of finance, health, resources and the environment, education, and human rights; the factors are income, inflation, demand for new jobs, urban population pressures, infant mortality, nutrition, clean water, energy use, adult literacy, and personal

Stanford University population expert Anne Ehrlich, who believes that uncontrolled population growth will lower living standards as more and more people try to share limited resources.

freedom. These are combined into a single rating for each country. The PCC applied the index to 130 countries and compared the results to annual rates of population increase. They found that countries with high rates of population increase also had high levels of suffering. The 30 countries that fell into the "extreme suffering" range had an average population increase of 2.8%, and so did the 44 countries that were ranked "high suffering." The index's "moderate suffering" range included 29 countries, with an average population increase of 1.7%. The 27 countries in the "minimal suffering" range had an average annual increase of 0.4%. The PCC concluded that "the correlation between rapid population growth and human suffering is consistent with other studies which indicate that rapid population increase restricts economic and social progress for individual families and nations."

Population growth is not the problem of the poor nations alone. Many people mistakenly believe that the populations of the United States and other industrialized countries have stopped growing. The *rate* of growth in the industrialized world has slowed, but growth is still taking place. Germany and Hungary were the only countries in the world whose populations did *not* become larger through natural increase in 1991 (but Germany's net population grew because of immigration into the country). The United States is the fastest-growing industrialized nation, with a 1991 birth rate of 17 and a natural increase rate of 0.8 (about half the global average rate, which was 1.7). In 1990, net U.S. population grew by about 2.4 million people, including natural increase and immigration.

Some Americans feel that the U.S. population should be growing faster. In his 1987 book *The Birth Dearth*, journalist Ben Wattenberg expressed alarm at the prospect of a world in which

"Western values" and "free Westerners" will be outnumbered by other population groups. Wattenberg's critics say that such fears emphasize ethnic and racial divisions at a time when it is crucial to forge new links of cooperation, tolerance, and understanding among different peoples. Wattenberg also claims that the United States needs a higher birth rate so that more young people will be available for military service, and so that there will be plenty of young workers to pay the costs of a growing number of elderly people (Social Security, Medicare, and so on). But others point out that modern military security depends more on technology than on the sheer number of soldiers, as was demonstrated by the 1991 Persian Gulf War, and that a high proportion of young people is as costly to society—in terms of schools, the juvenile justice system, day care, and social service programs such as welfare benefits—as a high proportion of older people.

The United States, Japan, the European countries, and other industrialized nations may be growing at a slower rate than the rest of the world, but they are using much more of the world's resources than the developing nations. The industrialized nations have 23% of the world's population and consume 80% of its resources. Many demographers predict that this gap will widen— that an ever-smaller proportion of people will consume an ever-larger amount of resources. The United States is a leader in disproportionate consumption. Americans account for about 5% of the world's population and use 28% of its energy, according to Zero Population Growth of Washington, D.C.

Paul Ehrlich and his colleagues have developed a formula for showing the impact made by different groups of people on the world's environment and its store of nonrenewable resources. The formula, which is described in *The Population*

Explosion, is I = PAT, or Impact equals Population times Affluence times Technology. This means that a population's mark on the environment is determined by three factors: the number of people; their average standard of consumption, or affluence; and the destructiveness of their technology. The levels of affluence and technology are low in China and India, but the population factors are very high, which means that these countries have a large impact on the global environment. The population factor is much smaller in the United States, but the levels of affluence and technology are quite high, so the overall impact is very great. Even a country with a relatively small population, such as Canada (26.8 million in 1991), can have a major impact because of its high levels of affluence and technology. There are four and a half times as many Nigerians in the world as Canadians, but very few Nigerians own automobiles, refrigerators, or central heating systems; Canada's impact is certainly equal to, and is probably much greater than, Nigeria's.

The I = PAT formula offers a way to evaluate the effects of different populations on the earth's ecosystem. Paul Ehrlich has calculated that every child born in the United States will have 2 times as much destructive impact on the environment as a Swedish child, 3 times as much as an Italian, 13 times as much as a Brazilian, 35 times as much as an Indian, 140 times as much as a Bangladeshi or Kenyan, and 280 times as much as a Chadian, Rwandan, Haitian, or Nepalese. One American birth thus contributes as much to the population crisis as 35 births in India, 140 in Kenya, or 280 in Haiti. Says Ehrlich, "These statistics should lay to rest the myth that population problems arise primarily from rapid growth in poor nations." He believes that the rich nations bear *at least* as much responsibility as the poor ones for finding solutions to population and environmental problems.

In a world that seems increasingly divided between the "haves" and the "have-nots," environmental and economic pressures related to overpopulation could cause new ethnic or international conflicts. The "water wars" mentioned in chapter 4 are one possibility. "Eco-refugees" are another potential source of conflict. If masses of people are driven by joblessness, famine, floods, or desertification to cross national borders, fighting may erupt between the refugees and their unwilling hosts over scarce resources.

Immigration is already a touchy subject in many countries. The late 1980s and early 1990s saw a rise in feeling against immigrants in Italy, France, Germany, Belgium, and other European nations as unemployment rose and economic conditions deteriorated. Some Europeans feel that the many Iranians, Africans, Turks, and others who have left their native countries to live and work in Europe are holding jobs and consuming resources that rightfully belong to Europeans. Antiforeigner sentiments have also been expressed by some Americans. Fears of excessive immigration are not limited to Western nations, however. Japan controls immigration very strictly, as does Singapore. And armed conflicts have broken out along the border between Bangladesh and the Indian state of Assam as desperate Bangladeshis flee across the border in search of a better life; similar tension exists along the border between Haiti and the Dominican Republic. Continued population growth—and the increased strain that it places on fragile environments and economies—is likely to make all of these pressures more acute.

As early as 1915, some groups of American women were advocating
birth control, not only to control population growth but to give women
more choices and freedom in their lives and careers.

chapter 6

P O P U L A T I O N   C O N T R O L

Those who believe that the earth's carrying capacity
is already being stressed, and that further population growth will
only make it more difficult to ensure that everyone's basic needs
are met, believe that population growth must be controlled. But
others think that the very question of population control is im-
moral or is a threat to individual freedoms. Religion and culture
deeply influence how many people feel about this complex and
sensitive issue. Perhaps no question in the world today is more
difficult to answer, or arouses stronger feelings on both sides, than
the question, "Should population growth be controlled?" The
question is a troubling one because it touches on some of humanity's most basic and private activities: sexual behavior, reproduction, and family life.

Population growth is controlled by limiting the number
of births. Birth control, sometimes called family planning, includes a variety of methods by which births can be prevented.
The most basic method of all—and the only completely effective
method—is refraining from sexual intercourse. Most people of
reproductive age, however, find this method unsatisfactory.
Sexually active couples can achieve birth control through

contraception, or the prevention of pregnancy. There are various types of contraception, with varying degrees of effectiveness. Both men and women can be sterilized, which does not affect sexual activity but prevents pregnancy altogether. Women can take medication in the form of pills or small implants under the skin; they can have intrauterine devices (IUDs) installed; or they can insert contraceptive aids such as diaphragms, sponges, or foams before having sex. Men can use condoms which have the added benefit of offering protection against AIDS and other sexually transmitted diseases. Each method has advantages and disadvantages; physicians and family planning specialists recommend that anyone who wants to practice contraception should receive information about the whole range of choices before deciding which method of birth control is best for him or her.

The final method of birth control is abortion, or ending a pregnancy by surgery or medication before the fetus is fully developed. Abortion is legal in some countries, illegal in others. In Russia, Poland, and many other countries where contraceptives are difficult to obtain, abortion has been used as a standard method of birth control. Yet even in countries where it is legal, such as the United States, abortion is a highly controversial issue. Many people are led by their religious or ethical beliefs to oppose it, not just for themselves but for others as well.

BARRIERS TO POPULATION CONTROL

Many factors work against the notion of population control. Some of these factors are religious. The Vatican, headquarters of the Roman Catholic church, officially opposes all types of birth control in the belief that preventing births goes against God's will. But many Catholics around the world, choosing to depart from the church's teaching in this matter, regularly practice birth control. Even in countries where Catholicism is the predominant faith, such as Italy and Mexico, birth control is in wide use. Although no other faith specifically forbids birth control practices, some other Christian sects and some groups of Islamic fundamentalists are against birth control; the members of these groups believe that they have a duty to increase their numbers rather than diminish them. Indeed, members of many cultural and ethnic groups around the world fear that if they limit population growth and other groups do not, their own group will be overwhelmed by other tribes, nationalities, or races that "outbreed" them. To these people, population control suggests a loss of ethnic, national, or racial identity.

Cultural traditions and values also work against population control in some places. In Islamic countries men are permitted to have up to four wives, and a man with multiple wives is expected to have children with each wife; one man may therefore father as many as several dozen children. The April 1991 issue of the *ZPG Reporter*, the newsletter of the Zero Population Growth organization, reported the case of Mehmet Sirin of Turkey, three of whose four wives were pregnant. Sirin and his wives already had 44 children. (Coincidentally, several months later the Turkish public television network allowed condoms to be advertised on television for the first time.)

Many cultures share the tradition of large families. Since the late 19th century, it has become quite common for North American and European families to have two children, or even a single child, but in many parts of the world five or six children is the norm. Families are larger in countries with high rates of infant mortality—this is to ensure that enough children will survive to adulthood to take care of the parents later on. Families also tend to be large in countries where the majority of people have traditionally been farmers, as children often provide the necessary labor in the family's fields or pastures. A related cultural value is the preference for sons over daughters; this is apparent in many cultures around the world. Traditionally, sons are expected to carry on the family name and to provide for their parents' old age, which means that male infants and children are often more highly prized than female ones. It is not uncommon for parents to have many children in order to have three or four sons.

Two other factors are very important in determining how people feel about population control and birth control. The first is education, and the second is the availability of contraceptives. Dozens of studies have shown that people with more education are more likely to understand and practice birth control. The level of a woman's education seems to be directly related to her fertility. A 1986 survey by the United Nations Educational, Scientific, and Cultural Organization (UNESCO) reported that in Sudan women with no formal education had an average of 6.5 children, those with four to six years of schooling had 5.0 children, and those with seven or more years of schooling had 3.4 children. In Mexico, women without education had an average of 8.0 children, but those with seven or more years of schooling had 2.7 children. Studies have also shown that people are more likely to favor population control if they have easy access to affordable family planning services and supplies. Pramilla Senanayake, assistant secretary-general of the International Planned Parenthood Federation (IPPF), is one of many who believe that women

The slums surrounding Nairobi, the capital city of Kenya, house tens of thousands of unemployed or underemployed people. At present birth rates, the population of Kenya will double in less than 20 years.

must have the opportunity to practice birth control if they wish to, if the quality of their lives is to improve. She says, "Millions of women are denied good health, education, and employment opportunities simply because they do not have the knowledge and the means to control their fertility."

THE STATUS OF WOMEN

One factor above all others determines how a given society responds to the issue of population control. That factor is the status of women within their society. Fertility—or the average number of children per woman—always drops when women are given more education, more job opportunities, and equal status with men.

Today fertility among European and North American women is the lowest in the world, with an average of 1.7 children per woman in Europe and 2.0 children per woman in the United States, as compared with 3.5 in Latin America, 3.9 in Asia, and 6.1 in Africa. But a century ago the fertility rate among Western women was much higher. The decline is due in large part to the increased status of women in Western society. As women achieved greater equality with men under the law, they began to marry later and to have smaller families. In country after country, the same pattern held: women with more education and more career opportunities tended to marry later, in their twenties instead of their teens, and they also tended to have fewer children. As a result, the rate of population growth in these countries slowed.

Demographers and social scientists believe that when women are able to seek fulfillment, self-expression, and financial independence through school and work, they feel less pressure to "prove" their worth to their husbands and families, or to society in general, by having many children. Paul and Anne Ehrlich point out in *The Population Explosion* that "when women have sources of status other than children, family sizes decline."

In some parts of the developing world, improvements in women's legal rights and educational opportunities have been accompanied by a drop in the fertility rate. Costa Rica, for example, has one of Central America's most successful school systems and a higher literacy rate than neighboring Central American countries. Its fertility rate is 3.3, compared to 4.1 for Central America as a whole.

Bangladesh is a good laboratory for testing the effect of changes in the status of women. It is the custom in that country for women to be married in their mid-teens and to have large families; a survey in the early 1980s showed that more than 60% of all Bangladeshi women had eight children or more. Cultural tradition makes Bangladeshi women subservient to men. Shazadio Harvum, dean of Bangladesh's School of Nursing, explains, "The prevailing attitude is that we women are meant for pain and suffering and the delivery of children. If we die in the process, that is no matter; he will take another wife. It must be realized that by custom the husband is superior, the wife inferior." Men outnumber women in every age group because the rate of female mortality is higher than the rate of male mortality. Many female babies die in infancy, possibly because they receive less care and nourishment than male babies—50% more girls than boys die between the ages of one and five, and many observers believe that some girl babies are deliberately neglected. Later in life, women are at high risk for death in childbirth (1 out of every 100 births results in the mother's death) or from botched at-home abortions (which kill 1 out of 3 women who undergo them).

In 1975 the government of Bangladesh introduced a revolutionary program of giving loans to village women to start small businesses, such as grocery stores or pottery works. More than 120,000 women formed cooperative associations to organize and operate their own businesses. They held weekly business meetings, and the government made family planning information and contraceptives available at these meetings. Several years later, the rate of contraceptive use among women who belonged to the co-op associations was 75%, while for the country as a whole it was less than 35%. This program and others like it have demon-

strated that when women are given access to education, employment, and family planning services, they voluntarily reduce their
fertility. But the program would have to be applied on a vastly
larger scale in order to have a significant effect on population
growth in Bangladesh, where the 1991 population was 116.6
million, the fertility rate was 4.9 (compared with 3.3 for Asia as a
whole), and the population *doubling time* was 28 years.

According to a report called *The Invisible Woman*,
prepared in 1990 by Zero Population Growth, women grow 50%
of the world's food and perform 66% of the world's work, yet
they earn only 10% of the world's income and own only 1% of
the world's property. In countries such as Nepal, Ethiopia,
Colombia, and Kenya, women perform a greater share of
agricultural work than men, yet they are banned by law from
owning land. Worldwide, women make up only 9.7% of all
national legislatures. Demographers and economists agree that
the key to economic development and a better way of life,
especially in the Third World, is population control. And
population control goes hand in hand with improving the legal,
economic, and political status of women. Says Nafis Sadik,
executive director of the United Nations Fund for Population
Activities (UNFPA), "More planners and policy makers must
recognize the contributions and the importance of women to
social and economic development."

POPULATION CONTROL CASE STUDIES

The question of population control is a vexing one for
governments. Each of them answers it in its own way. Many

countries, including the United States, have no formal population policy. Other nations have created official programs to deal with population growth. These programs use a wide range of methods and have yielded varying degrees of success.

The world's strictest, most controversial, and most successful population control program is that of China, the world's most populous country. In 1991 it had 1.1 billion people and a doubling time of 48 years. In China, birth control is a matter of law. In 1979, appalled by a rapid rate of population growth that was projected to reach 1.8 billion people by the year 2000, the Chinese government introduced its "one family, one child" policy. Parents who have more than one child are subject to certain financial and social penalties, which can include annual fines for up to 16 years, reductions in their salaries, refusal of requests to have their housing space or food rations increased, compulsory sterilization for one of the parents, and bearing the full cost of the extra child's medical care and education. (Ethnic minorities and people in some rural districts are permitted to have two or three children.)

China's population control program has become controversial in the Western world because of reports that some women have been forced to undergo abortions. Although such abuses have occurred, they are not part of China's national policy, which allows abortion but forbids local officials from forcing it on unwilling women. There have also been reports that some parents have neglected or even killed baby girls in order that the one permitted child would be a boy.

To Westerners, who share a cultural tradition that values personal freedom above society's well-being, China's strict, coercive policy often appears to violate individual rights. Yet many Westerners are unaware that that policy is the government's response to an extraordinary disaster—the mass starvation of 30 million Chinese in famines that ravaged the land from 1958 to 1962. China's leaders believe that they must halt population growth in order to prevent a similar tragedy in the future. And Chinese society as a whole is paying a heavy price for population growth. China suffers from chronic food and water shortages, as well as environmental degradation and pollution on a massive scale. The country's long-term carrying capacity is estimated to be about 700 million people, far fewer than the current population.

China's program has made a difference. The fertility rate has dropped from 5.5 in 1960 to 2.3 in 1991. Instead of the 1.8 billion people that demographers in 1979 projected for the year 2000, China is now expected to have 1.3 billion in that year. The difference is half a billion people—twice as many as the entire U.S. population.

On the other hand, India, the second most populous country in the world (859.2 million in 1991), has failed dismally in its attempt to control population growth. In 1952, India started the developing world's first official family planning program. In the 40 years since then, however, the program has not been very effective, possibly because family planning has not been integrated into a well-funded, nationwide program to improve education, the health of mothers and children, and the status of women. One feature of the program was cash payments to adults who volunteered to be sterilized. But in 1975, Prime Minister Indira Gandhi declared that all parents with three or more children should be sterilized, and the government used a great deal of pressure—even force, in some cases—to carry out her decree. Some 8 million sterilizations, mostly on women, were performed in the following two years. But people responded to this heavy-handed approach with fear and anger, and the program was extremely unpopular; it was one of the reasons that Gandhi was voted out of office in 1977. Since then the government has tried to encourage contraceptive use by emphasizing the rewards of small families on television, radio, and billboards, but to many people contraceptives and family planning information are not readily available. India's population is now expected to reach 1 billion by the year 2000 and to surpass China's by the middle of the 21st century.

The fastest-growing country in the world is Kenya. In 1960, Kenya's population was 9.5 million, and its rate of natural increase was 3.3%. In 1991, Kenya had a population of 25.2 million and an increase rate of 3.8%. If that rate of growth continues, Kenya's population will have doubled to 50.4 million by the year 2009. Farmland is being eroded and desertified, and people are flocking to the cities. Nairobi, the capital, is growing at the rate of 8% a year. The burgeoning slums of Kenya's cities do not offer a much brighter prospect than the bleak countryside, however; 2 million people, about 20% of the work force, are unemployed. The government supports family planning and wants to control population growth, but a deeply rooted tradition of large families among the various tribes of Kenya has made the Kenyan people slow to accept the idea of limiting their families; in 1991 Kenyan women had a fertility rate of 6.7 children per woman. Many Kenyans are suspicious of attempts to control population growth—in 1986 thousands of schoolchildren refused to drink milk supplied by government aid programs because of rumors that the milk contained contraceptives. Some Kenyans also believe that Western nations that encourage birth control simply want to dominate Africans by keeping their numbers down.

Other developing nations, however, have been much more successful in slowing their growth rates. By increasing family planning education at the community level and giving free contraceptives to anyone who requested them, Indonesia raised the number of couples who practice birth control from 400,000 to 18.6 million between 1972 and 1989; the nation's fertility rate dropped from 5.6 to 3.4 during the same period. Mexico's fertility rate dropped from 7.2 in 1960 to 3.8 in 1991, thanks in part to Mexico's 1974 constitution, which gave women equal rights with men and guaranteed free birth control to all. Since the mid-1970s, the Mexican government has regarded family planning as one of the country's top priorities. The population is still growing, but it is growing at a slower rate than that of any other Central American country except Panama.

Thailand has also experienced some success with family planning, partly because of one man's efforts. In 1974, economist Mechai Viravaidya founded Thailand's Population and Community Development Association. Since then he has used a number of zany stunts to call attention to family planning. Viravaidya has sponsored balloon-blowing contests with condoms, distributed condoms in traffic jams and at movie theaters, and passed out T-shirts reading "A Condom a Day Keeps the Doctor Away." As a result of his highly visible promotion of condoms for both birth control and safe sex, condoms are now often called "mechais" in Thailand. He has also persuaded the government that population control and economic development must be linked—for example, by giving more agricultural aid to farmers who sign an agreement to limit their family size. Viravaidya's efforts have paid off. In 1970 Thailand's growth rate was 3.2%. By 1991 it had fallen to 1.3%, the lowest in Southeast Asia.

Different countries have developed a variety of ways to encourage population control. Some methods use incentives—that is, financial or other benefits to keep family size within the recommended limits. For example, governments may make one-time payments to people who undergo sterilization or to doctors who perform sterilizations. Or they may make periodic payments into the savings accounts or retirement funds of parents who keep their families under a certain limit. Other incentives include special privileges, such as better housing, for smaller families. Some countries, like China, use disincentives—that is, penalties to those who exceed the recommended family size. South Korea and Pakistan do not allow tax deductions for families with more than two children. In Singapore, families who have more than three children are not allowed to receive certain benefits, such as admission to the best schools. In some countries, employers do not provide women with maternity leave and benefits beyond a certain number of children.

The question of how far governments should go in shaping the family lives of their citizens will no doubt continue to be urgently debated in all parts of the world. But experts who have studied the population control programs of various countries claim that nations that wish to control the growth of their populations have a better chance of doing so if:

- Birth control is introduced and promoted in ways that are designed to mesh with people's cultures and traditions as much as possible.
- Family planning services, including basic health care and a variety of contraceptive choices, are available to

everyone, which means that they must be provided free to those who cannot afford to pay for them.

- Public education campaigns encourage people to use contraceptives by focusing on the financial and health advantages of small families.
- Economic and social development programs are aimed at improving literacy, reducing infant mortality rates, and increasing employment.

As the chart shows, even small changes in fertility rates can have far-reaching consequences in terms of controlling population.

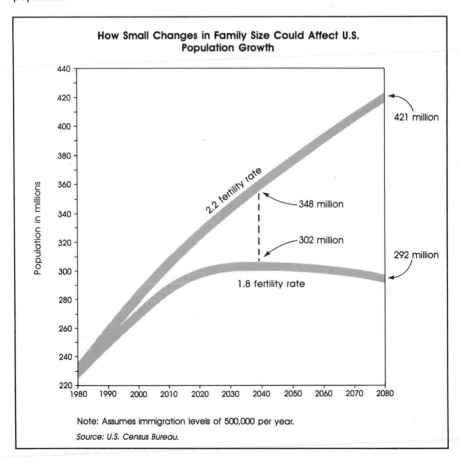

How Small Changes in Family Size Could Affect U.S. Population Growth

Note: Assumes immigration levels of 500,000 per year.

Source: U.S. Census Bureau.

- Social services include pensions and health care, so that people do not need to rear large families to provide for them in their later years.
- Women are recognized by the law as equal to men, and they have equal access to education, loans, ownership of land and property, benefits of aid and development programs, and jobs.

THE ROLE OF THE UNITED STATES

For many years, the United States was a leader in the international family planning movement, donating large sums to the United Nations Fund for Population Activities (UNFPA) and the International Planned Parenthood Federation (IPPF), the world's largest organizations devoted to family planning. In the early 1970s, the United States gave high priority to global population control. George Bush was head of the Republican Task Force on Population and Earth Resources in the U.S. House of Representatives when he wrote, in 1973: "Today, the population problem is no longer a private matter. In a world of nearly 4 billion people increasing by 2%, or 80 million more, every year, population growth and how to restrain it are public concerns that command the attention of national and international leaders."

During the presidency of Ronald Reagan, however, the United States abandoned its position of leadership on the issue of population control. Largely because of pressure from activists who confused the general question of population control with the specific issue of abortion, the Reagan administration withdrew funding from IPPF in 1985 and from UNFPA in 1986. U.S. funding for international family planning efforts fell by 20% between 1985 and 1987. Since then the United States, one of the fastest-growing industrialized nations, has not formulated a population policy of its own, nor has it officially taken part in international discussions of the population crisis.

By 1989, George Bush had become president of the United States. That year he vetoed a bill that would have restored U.S. funding to population assistance programs under UNFPA. As with the Reagan administration, the Bush administration has declined to fund UNFPA because antiabortion activists, many of them members of Bush's own Republican party, claim that UNFPA has supported forced abortions for women in China. According to Zero Population Growth and UNFPA, however,

Lester Brown, president of the Worldwatch Institute, has made the point that however difficult it may be to curtail individual reproductive rights and control population growth, living in a world where such growth is not controlled will be even more difficult.

UNFPA aid has accounted for less than 1% of the cost of China's population program, mostly in the form of computers and demographic surveys.

But if population control is no longer a priority to the leadership of the United States, it is a source of great concern to other world leaders. More than 40 heads of government, representing more than half the population of the world, signed a Statement on Population Stabilization in 1985. The statement said, "Degradation of the world's environment, income inequality and the potential for conflict exist today because of over-consumption and overpopulation." Calling on all countries to join in an international population control effort, the statement continued, "Recognizing that early population stabilization is in the interest of all nations, we earnestly hope that leaders around the world will share our views and join us in this great undertaking for the well-being and happiness of people everywhere."

Controlling the growth of the world's population means, very simply, that people will have to have fewer children. Finding ways to control population that are fair to everyone, and that respect the rights of all people, may be the most serious challenge that the human race has ever faced. Lester Brown of the Worldwatch Institute says of the need to control population growth, "It is hard to imagine anything more difficult . . . except suffering the consequences of failing to do so."

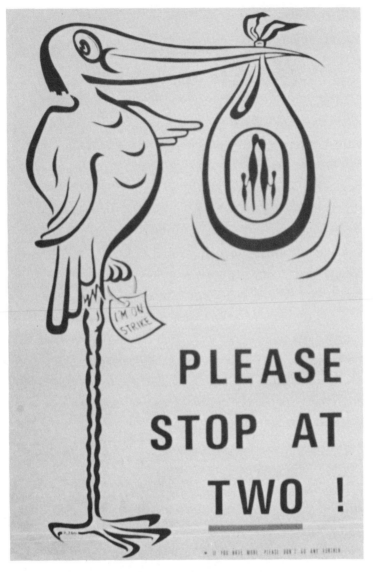

A family planning poster from the government of Singapore, where hospitals impose heavy increases in the cost of maternity care for families having more than the recommended number of children.

O V E R P O P U L A T I O N
T O D A Y   A N D   T O M O R R O W

The earth's population is growing at the rate of 1.7% per year. The greatest increase is occurring in Africa, which is growing at the rate of 3.0% and will double its 1991 population of 677 million by the year 2014. Africa's population-related woes are so grave that the Ehrlichs, authors of *The Population Explosion*, call that continent "a demographic basket case." Latin America has the next-highest growth rate, 2.1%. The total 1991 population of the Latin American countries was 451 million and is scheduled to double by 2025. Asia's overall growth rate is 1.8% (2.0% if China is left out). Its 1991 population of 3.1 billion will double by 2029 if this rate of growth continues.

Australia and the Pacific Ocean islands had a population of 27 million in 1991 (17.5 million in Australia alone). With a growth rate of 1.2, the region's population will double by 2051. North America and the former Soviet Union have the same growth rate, 0.8%. North America's 1991 population of 280 million will double by 2079; the 292 million former Soviets will double their numbers by 2082.

The world's slowest-growing region is Europe, with a 1991 population of 502 million and a growth rate of 0.2%. At that rate, Europe's population will not double itself until the year 2284. Europe contains the only nation in the world whose population is shrinking—Hungary, where the death rate was 14 and the birth rate was 12 in 1991,—as well as the only nation in the world that has achieved zero population growth—Germany, where the birth and death rates were both 11 in 1991.

Most demographers and environmentalists, however, urge that people in all countries must learn to regard overpopulation not as a national or regional issue but as a global issue. The problems caused by overpopulation—including deforestation, global warming, and species extinction—affect the whole planet, and any real solution to the population problem will also have to be international in nature.

Population experts from many organizations and parts of the world have declared that zero population growth should be every country's goal (many of them go still further and say that population size should shrink). But demographers warn that even if every new family on earth limited its size to two children starting next year, the world's population would still continue to rise for decades. Two factors—*age composition* and *demographic momentum*—guarantee it.

Age composition refers to how a given population is divided into age groups. For example, Europe's age composition is quite different from Africa's. Europe has a higher percentage of people over 65 and a lower percentage of people under 15 than Africa. Demographic momentum refers to the fact that population growth has a momentum, or moving force, of its own. A population that is growing will keep on growing for several generations, even if people immediately limit their reproduction to the replacement rate of one child for each parent, because people who are now young will grow up and live side by side with their children and grandchildren before they begin to die. Therefore, the total number of people in the world will continue to grow for about 50 years, while the average age of the population increases. After several generations, the death rate will begin to equal the birth rate, and growth will level off. Only if death rates rose suddenly and drastically could a growing population reach instant zero population growth.

Demographic momentum means that population growth cannot be stopped in its tracks. Even the most drastic birth control measures will not produce instant results. The best that can be hoped for is that population growth will slow to a halt in 50 or 60 years—and that will happen only if birth rates drop quickly and

Another family planning poster from Singapore. Singapore has one of the lowest birth rates in Asia outside of China. In fact, recent concerns about having a large enough labor force have prompted the government to modify its policies and encourage marriage at an earlier age.

small families have more to eat

Singapore wants all married couples to have no more than two children so that there will be food, work, a home and security for everyone. Call at your nearest Family Planning Clinic where doctors will explain how safe and simple it is to keep your family small.

THIS ADVICE IS PRIVATE AND FREE

dramatically. During the 1990s, 3 billion people around the world will reach the age of 15 and enter their reproductive years. The reproductive decisions of these young men and women will determine whether the earth's population levels off at around 10 billion in the 21st century, as the most optimistic projections say that it will, or soars to 14 billion or even more. The Worldwatch Institute's Lester Brown is thinking of demographic momentum when he speaks of the need to control population growth: "Time is not on our side. We have years, not decades, to turn the situation around. And even then there is no guarantee that we will be able to reverse the trends that are undermining the human prospect, but if we do it will be during the 1990s."

WHAT EVERYONE CAN DO NOW

If it is true that population growth threatens both the natural world and human civilization, as many environmentalists, demographers, and economists believe, it is also true that people can control that growth. Slowing or halting population growth will take time and will require concern, commitment, and cooperation on the part of individuals and governments around the world. Here are some things that you can do:

- Inform yourself. Read about various aspects of the population problem. Weigh the arguments of those who support population control *and* those who are against it, and decide for yourself how you feel about the issue.
- Discuss population and environmental problems with a variety of people: your family, teachers and classmates, and religious and community leaders.

- Make overpopulation the subject of a school report or project. Zero Population Growth has a number of suggestions for projects dealing with population, world hunger, and the environment.
- Examine the statements of your government representatives to see where they stand on the issue of family planning. Write to your congressperson or senator expressing your views on population growth and birth control.
- Study the publications of such groups as the Population Institute and Zero Population Growth. If you agree with a group's goals, you can subscribe to its newsletter, make a donation, or offer your services as a volunteer.
- Reduce your impact on the global environment. Recycle. Cut down on unnecessary water use. Take part in a tree-planting project (the Audubon Society, Sierra Club, and other environmental groups sponsor such activities in many locations). Learn about nutrition, and experiment with healthy vegetarian meals several times a week. Many books with lists of everyday conservation steps are available in bookstores and libraries.
- Respect the decisions of people who choose not to have children or who choose to limit their family size.
- Above all, make informed and responsible decisions about your own reproductive behavior.

The organizations listed in the Appendix can provide you with more information about overpopulation, population and the environment, and population control.

APPENDIX: FOR MORE INFORMATION

Carrying Capacity
1325 G Street NW
Suite 1003
Washington, DC 20005
(202) 879-3045

Center for Population Options
1012 14th Street NW
Suite 1200
Washington, DC 20005
(202) 347-5700

Food and Agriculture
   Organization of the United
   Nations
1001 22nd Street NW
Suite 300
Washington, DC 20002
(202) 653-2398

Negative Population Growth
210 The Plaza
Teaneck, NJ 07666
(201) 837-3555

Population Crisis Committee
1120 19th Street NW
Suite 550
Washington, DC 20036
(202) 659-1833

Population-Environment Balance
1325 G Street NW

Suite 1003
Washington, DC 20005-3104
(202) 879-3000

Population Institute
110 Maryland Avenue NE
Suite 207
Washington, DC 20002
(202) 544-3300

Population Reference Bureau,
   Inc.
1875 Connecticut Avenue
Suite 520
Washington, DC 20009-5728
(202) 483-1100

Population Resources Center
500 East 62nd Street
New York, NY 10021
(212) 888-2820

United Nations Fund for
   Population Activities
220 East 42nd Street
New York, NY 10017
(212) 279-5000

Zero Population Growth
1400 16th Street NW
Suite 320
Washington, DC 20036
(202) 332-2200

FURTHER READING

Alan Shawn Feinstein World Hunger Program. *The Hunger Report.* Providence, RI: Brown University Press, 1988.

Alonso, William, ed. *Population in an Interacting World.* Cambridge: Harvard University Press, 1987.

Brown, Lester. *Building a Sustainable Society.* New York: Norton, 1981.

————. *State of the World, 1991.* New York: Norton, 1991.

————. *The Twenty-ninth Day: Accommodating Human Needs and Numbers to the Earth's Resources.* New York: Norton, 1978.

Camp, Sharon, and Joseph Spiedel. *The International Human Suffering Index.* Washington, DC: Population Crisis Committee, 1987.

Caplan, Ruth. *Our Earth, Ourselves.* New York: Bantam Books, 1990.

Ehrlich, Paul. *The Machinery of Nature.* New York: Simon & Schuster, 1986.

————. *The Population Bomb.* New York: Ballantine Books, 1968.

Ehrlich, Paul, and Anne Ehrlich. *Earth.* New York: Watts, 1987.

————. *The Population Explosion.* New York: Simon & Schuster, 1990.

Fornos, Werner. *Gaining People, Losing Ground: A Blueprint for Stabilizing World Population.* Washington, DC: Population Institute, 1987.

Fraser, Dean. *The People Problem: What You Should Know About Growing Population and Vanishing Resources.* Chicago: Greenwood, 1983.

George, Susan. *How the Other Half Dies: The Real Reasons for World Hunger.* Montclair, NJ: Allenheld, Osmun, 1977.

Global Tomorrow Coalition. *The Global Ecology Handbook.* Boston: Beacon Press, 1990.

Gupte, Pranay. *The Crowded Earth: People and the Politics of Population.* New York: Norton, 1984.

Harrison, Paul. *The Greening of Africa.* New York: Penguin Books, 1987.

Kangas, George. *Population and Survival: The Challenge in Five Countries.* Chicago: Greenwood, 1984.

McNeill, William. *Plagues and Peoples.* New York: Doubleday, 1976.

Menken, Jane, ed. *World Population and U.S. Policy: The Choices Ahead.* New York: Norton, 1986.

Morris, David. *Measuring the Condition of the World's Poor: The Physical Quality of Life Index.* New York: Pergamon Press, 1979.

Nam, Charles. *Think About Our Population: The Changing Face of America.* New York: Walker, 1988.

Ornstein, Robert, and Paul Ehrlich. *New World, New Mind.* New York: Simon & Schuster, 1989.

Reining, Priscilla, and Irene Tinker, eds. *Population: Dynamics, Ethics, and Policy.* Washington, DC: American Association for the Advancement of Science, 1975.

Robinson, Harry. *Population and Resources*. New York: St. Martin's, 1982.

Santos, Miguel. *Managing Planet Earth: Perspectives on Population, Ecology and the Law*. Chicago: Greenwood, 1990.

Simon, Julian. *The Ultimate Resource*. Princeton, NJ: Princeton University Press, 1981.

Stefoff, Rebecca. *Extinction*. New York: Chelsea House, 1991.

Steger, Will, and Jon Bowermaster. *Saving the Earth: A Citizen's Guide to Environmental Action*. New York: Knopf, 1990.

Stwertka, Eve, and Albert Stwertka. *Population: Growth, Change, and Impact*. New York: Watts, 1981.

United Nations Fund for Population Activities. *Population Policies and Programs*. New York: New York University Press, 1991.

United States Commission on Population Growth and the American Future. *Population and the American Future*. Washington, DC: U.S. Government Printing Office, 1972.

Wattenberg, Ben. *The Birth Dearth: What Happens When People in Free Countries Don't Have Enough Babies*. New York: Pharos Books, 1987.

Weiner, Jonathan. *The Next One Hundred Years: Shaping the Fate of Our Living Earth*. New York: Bantam Books, 1990.

Winckler, Suzanne. *Our Endangered Planet*. Minneapolis: Lerner, 1991.

World Commission on Environment and Development. *Our Common Future*. Oxford: Oxford University Press, 1988.

GLOSSARY

age composition   A population's composition by age groups.

aquifer   Porous underground rock or a rock formation that creates a natural underground reservoir that holds groundwater.

birth rate   The number of people born each year for every 1,000 people in a given population, whether of the earth as a whole or of a particular country, region, or city.

carrying capacity   The number of inhabitants that a particular area—the earth, a country, or a certain ecosystem—can support over a long period of time without having its environment permanently damaged and without irreplaceable loss of its resources.

death rate   The number of people who die each year for every 1,000 people in a given population; also known as mortality rate.

demographic momentum   The fact that a growing population will continue to grow larger for some years even if its fertility rate drops immediately to the level of replacement reproduction. Demographic momentum is caused by two demographic facts: first, births take place among younger people and deaths take place among older people; second, growing populations tend to have more young people than old people, more births than deaths.

demographics   The statistical characteristics of a given population.

demography   The study of population size, density, and distribution.

distribution   How a population is geographically spread over an area; usually expressed as the percentage of a population that is urban and the percentage that is rural.

doubling time   The number of years until a given population doubles if the growth rate remains the same.

fertility rate   The average number of children that a woman in a given population will have, if the **birth rate** for her age group does not change.

infant mortality rate   The number of children who die before reaching one year of age for every 1,000 live births.

life expectancy   The average number of years that a newborn infant in a particular population can be expected to live, if the **death rate** does not change.

migration   The movement of people from one country, place, or locality to another.

natural increase   The difference between the birth rate and the death .rate, expressed as a percentage; sometimes called rate of natural increase.

net migration   The difference between the number of immigrants and the number of emigrants; the number of people added to or lost from a population as a result of migration.

net population growth   The actual number of people added to a population in a given period of time; the sum of **natural increase** and **net migration**.

pronatalist   Favoring high fertility and a high birth rate.

replacement reproduction rate   The fertility rate at which each couple is replaced by just two descendants, and population does not increase.

INDEX

ABOUT THE AUTHOR

REBECCA STEFOFF is a Philadelphia-based writer and editor who has published more than 40 nonfiction books for young adults. Many of her books deal with geography and exploration, and she takes an active interest in environmental issues and global ecology. She has also served as the editorial director of two Chelsea House series—*Places and Peoples of the World* and *Let's Discover Canada* series. Stefoff received her M.A. and Ph.D. degrees in English from the University of Pennsylvania, where she taught for three years.

ABOUT THE EDITOR

RUSSELL E. TRAIN, currently chairman of the board of directors of the World Wildlife Fund and The Conservation Foundation, has had a long and distinguished career of government service under three presidents. In 1957 President Eisenhower appointed him a judge of the United States Tax Court. He served Lyndon Johnson on the National Water Commission. Under Richard Nixon he became under secretary of the Interior and, in 1970, first chairman of the Council on Environmental Quality. From 1973 to 1977 he served as administrator of the Environmental Protection Agency. Train is also a trustee or director of the African Wildlife Foundation; the Alliance to Save Energy; the American Conservation Association; Citizens for Ocean Law; Clean Sites, Inc.; the Elizabeth Haub Foundation; the King Mahendra Trust for Nature Conservation (Nepal); Resources for the Future; the Rockefeller Brothers Fund; the Scientists' Institute for Public Information; the World Resources Institute; and Union Carbide and Applied Energy Services, Inc. Train is a graduate of Princeton and Columbia Universities, a veteran of World War II, and currently resides in the District of Columbia.